Using a Multisensory Environment

A Practical Guide for Teachers

Paul Pagliano

David Fulton Publishers
London

David Fulton Publishers Ltd
Ormond House, 26–27 Boswell Street, London WC1N 3JZ

www.fultonpublishers.co.uk

First published in Great Britain by David Fulton Publishers 2001

British Library Cataloguing in Publication Data
A catalogue record for this book is available from the British Library

ISBN 1–85346–716–2

The publishers would like to thank Christine Avery for copy-editing and Sheila Harding for proofreading this book.

Typeset by Elite Typesetting Techniques, Eastleigh, Hampshire
Printed in Great Britain by Bell and Bain Ltd, Glasgow.

Contents

Acknowledgements

I would like to thank the students and staff of Mundingburra Special School for inviting me to be part of their Multisensory Environment team. It was the practical experience I gained during my sessions in the Mundingburra Special School MSE which was the foundation of this book. In particular I would like to thank the staff for their generous feedback on my assessment forms. Thanks also to Kate Bishop in Sydney, Kim Talbot at Arohanui Special School, Auckland, New Zealand and Susan Fowler, Spastic Society of Victoria, Melbourne. Our discussions regarding therapy, design and the built environment helped me shape my understanding of how the MSE could work in practice.

Writing this book was partially funded by a research grant. This 2000 Merit Research Grant through James Cook University allowed me to collect data on how MSEs are used in practice. Thanks Paula Geldens, my research assistant for your ongoing support. Even though the vignettes I provide in this book have been informed by my research, they have been fictionalised to protect the identity of the children involved and to illustrate more clearly the principles under discussion.

Thanks to my School of Education at James Cook University in Townsville for making time available for me to write this book through their Special Studies Program. Thanks to my excellent hosts in North America: to the staff and students of the Faculty of Education at Malaspina University College, British Columbia and at the Virginia Sowell Center for Visual Impairment, Texas Tech University, Lubbock, Texas. In particular I wish to thank Dr Pat Kelley for her encouragement and critical comments. Thanks also to my colleagues in the South Pacific Educators in Vision Impairment. The support I have received from this association has been invaluable.

Finally I wish to acknowledge the very substantial assistance I have received from my wife and children. My wife, Dr Fiona McWhinnie, has proofread and criticised every draft of this book and has spent many hours working behind the scenes to ensure it got to final product. Without her support and friendship I would not have been able to write this book.

1 The MSE: equipment, resources and outcomes

Introduction

Every child develops and learns in his or her own unique way, through interacting with the particular environment he or she lives in. When a child is able bodied, interaction is spontaneous and natural, so that the relationship between the child's development and the environment is generally taken for granted. Only a highly deprived environment will stunt the child's biologically predetermined progression through the developmental milestones.

A sense impairment compromises development, because necessary prerequisites to the next stage of learning may not have been laid down. A profound impairment can impede the spontaneous and natural process of development and learning to such an extent that, unless the environment is shaped in certain ways to be supportive, the child will have great difficulty making sense of the world.

In a multisensory environment (MSE) stimulation of a multisensory nature is precisely shaped to match the exceptional multisensory needs of the user. Essentially the goal is to enable the user to make more purposeful use of his or her remaining sense abilities.

The MSE can be used with a wide range of individuals. However, the particular focus of this book is to consider the use of the MSE with children with profound multiple learning difficulties (PMLD).

Where did the multisensory environment (MSE) come from?

The evolution of the multisensory environment can be traced back to three separate technological and sociological changes that occurred in the 1970s. These developments were the discotheque, soft play equipment and new services for people with disabilities (Hirstwood and Gray 1995).

The emergence of the discotheque was a high point in the use of industrial psychology to create a multisensory environment for entertainment. Loud rhythmic music coupled with sophisticated, sound-activated lighting helped create an environment with an exciting visual and aural ambience.

Miniaturisation made the discotheque portable. Equipment became relatively cheap and accessible. Accompanying the technological developments was a sociological change in expectations. The use of environmental effects to create atmosphere for a set purpose, particularly entertainment, became commonplace and accepted.

The 1970s also witnessed a steady increase in the number of mothers returning to work soon after childbirth. The resultant burgeoning child care industry created increased demand for safe, all-weather play environments that were stimulating and meaningful for very young children yet easy to clean and maintain. In parallel with these sociological changes were important technological developments in the plastics industry. These included:

- the popularisation of PVC, a lightweight, waterproof, synthetic material which could be used to cover foam rubber to make construction shapes and soft furnishings;
- the invention of Velcro, a material which could provide strong, easy, instant fastening and unfastening;
- the appearance of large shape, hard plastic moulding for the manufacture of lightweight, colourful, sturdy playground equipment.

Nowadays toyshops are filled with a seemingly limitless variety of soft play equipment.

Services for individuals with disabilities also underwent considerable change in the 1970s. These included:

- deinstitutionalisation, the process of moving individuals with disabilities out of institutions into society;
- mainstreaming, the process of moving children with disabilities out of segregated special schools into regular schools (the least restrictive environment) for the purpose of education with their nondisabled peers;
- normalisation, the process of making the life and environment of individuals with disabilities as normal as possible.

Educational and social services replaced the medical model, where disability is assumed to be a disease or condition which requires amelioration, with the ecological model, where emphasis is placed on viewing the individual in complex interaction with the environment. The professional as expert was similarly reframed as the professional as collaborator and team player, whose goal is to assist the individual with the disability to become as self-determining as possible. These changes were seen as keys to ensuring that people with disabilities achieve a higher quality of life.

The MSE arose from these three developments for the following reasons. The discotheque provided the technological know-how to create exciting multisensory environments. The discotheque also changed social expectations regarding the use of environmental effects within the built environment. The development of soft play environments meant these environments could now be made to suit even the most rudimentary of ability levels yet still remain safe, easy to clean, all-weather places.

Deinstitutionalisation, mainstreaming and normalisation helped make life for people with disabilities more like that for the nondisabled population. The move from the medical model to the ecological model helped emphasise the importance of age and level-appropriate environments that were stimulating and meaningful for the person with the disability, where the individual could show preferences and exercise free choice.

Snoezelen

In the late 1970s a series of sensory rooms (tactual, aural, visual, ball bath, water, smell and taste) were created at the De Hartenberg Centre in The Netherlands. These rooms were for relaxation and stimulation, hence their name, 'snoezelen' a contraction of the Dutch words 'snuffelen' to smell and 'doezelen' to doze. Hulsegge and Verheul wrote about these 'snoezelen' rooms in their book *Snoezelen: Another World* (1986 Dutch, 1987 English). The 'snoezelen' combined the visual and aural ambience of the discotheque with soft play furnishings to create multisensory environments.

Hulsegge and Verheul's (1986/7) 'snoezelen' philosophy was based on the premise that an appeal to primary sensations was a more immediately powerful means of contacting a person with severe disability than any initial appeal to intellectual capabilities. Their 'snoezelen' was essentially a place for recreation where learning was viewed as being of secondary or incidental importance. The emphasis was on the person with the disability being in control with a nondisabled person as the facilitator. When communication difficulties made the likes and preferences of the person with a disability unclear, facilitators were encouraged to carefully observe and adopt a 'critical attitude' (p. 10) regarding their observations of the person in the 'snoezelen'.

Active centres or dumping grounds?

Hulsegge and Verheul (1986/7) criticised their own work saying it lacked 'a solid theoretical basis' to guide and inform 'snoezelen' use. Furthermore they stated that their philosophy lacked 'uniformity' (p. 127).

For example, on the one hand the authors argued that '"Snoezelen" is an activity where 'expertise' is not absolutely necessary' (p. 116), yet on the other hand, they emphasised the need for 'careful observation [of the person with PMLD]… in order to recognize, register and translate signals' (p. 126). The authors thought the facilitators needed to rely on 'intuition' yet needed to maintain a 'critical attitude' (p. 10). The authors also claimed 'Learning is not a must, but they [the individuals with PMLD] should be given the opportunity to gain experience' (p. 23).

The theoretical vacuum and the internal inconsistencies resulted in serious problems of interpretation. This in turn resulted in a range of 'snoezelen' experiences from good to bad. Kewin (1991) identified the good in terms of improved relationships between the facilitator and the user:

As relationships between users and helpers develop within Snoezelen and we focus more on sensory experience and communication, there can be a freeing up of carer/participant relationships. People are more readily accepted as interesting in their own right as we learn much more about their likes and dislikes.

At the other end of the spectrum Hopkins and Willetts (1993) observed, 'When these places are badly used, the children become passive and confused by competing stimuli, causing them to retreat into a withdrawn state' (p. 26).

Not all 'snoezelen' facilitators bothered to facilitate. Some staff simply used the facility as a space to place individuals with disabilities and leave them. This abuse of the 'snoezelen' led Mount and Cavet (1995) to caution that:

… in the absence of rigorous research the value of multi-sensory environments will be over-estimated and, in the present situation, may be regarded as active treatment centres when, in fact, they are being used for containment, or as dumping ground where people with learning difficulties are placed and ignored. (p. 54)

An opportunity to make money

The 'snoezelen' concept also provided opportunity for the emergence of an MSE industry. This industry consists of a number of commercial interests, some good, some well meaning, and some seemingly more motivated by making money or seduced by the means (the multisensory 'big boy toys' and equipment) than by a genuine desire to achieve valued outcomes for individuals with disabilities.

I have therefore endeavoured to distance myself from all commercial interests associated with the MSE industry (my apologies to those who are providing a high quality service). My goal in writing this book is to provide information to practitioners working in the field that will enable them to become increasingly discriminating and in control of the way MSEs are used and less susceptible to the sales pitch of unscrupulous merchants. I am working on the assumption that the better informed the practitioners are, the better they will be at working out which commercial interests provide value for money and which do not.

Two approaches

In spite of the difficulties, the 'snoezelen' concept spread around the world in the late 1980s and early 90s and was adopted by a range of services for people with disabilities both community and educational. The 'snoezelen' became particularly popular in special schools for children with PMLD. Some special schools maintained the original 'snoezelen' philosophy with its primary emphasis on recreation but others reinterpreted the philosophy to make education the primary emphasis.

According to Hirstwood and Smith (1996) 'a philosophical rivalry' arose between the two approaches. Bozic (1997) highlighted the differences between them in research he conducted in special schools in England where the original 'snoezelen' philosophy was described as 'a child-led repertoire' or passive approach, and the education philosophy was described as a 'developmental repertoire' or interactive approach.

An 'open-minded' space

Hirstwood and Smith (1996) believed that the two approaches could be used together and argued for a more flexible use of the space. The term 'snoezelen', which had become the registered trade mark of the UK company ROMPA, began to be replaced by the term MSE. This new term helped unshackle the MSE from the narrow or single function definitions imposed by the opposing 'snoezelen' philosophies and freed up the way the MSE could be defined.

This led Pagliano (1998) to argue that the MSE is a multifunctional space. Multiple functions relate to clients (young infant to aged adult, profound multiple disability to dementia), facilitators (teachers, therapists, parents, caregivers, psychologists, social workers and nurses) and purpose (leisure, therapy and education). The 'single-minded' single function space concept of the 'snoezelen' has been superseded by what Walzer classifies as an 'open-minded' space (Rogers 1997), an MSE that embraces plurality and variety of interaction. Figure 1.1 shows this evolution of the 'open-minded' MSE.

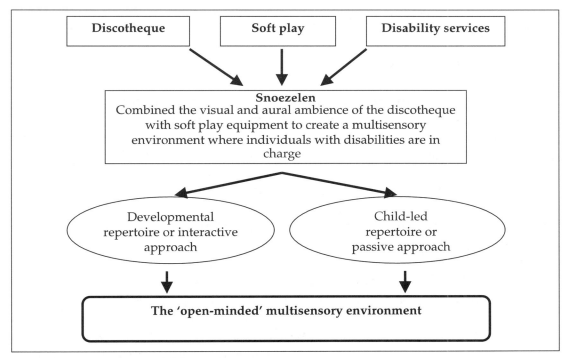

Figure 1.1 Evolution of the MSE

Why fashion stimulation to match the child's needs?

The natural environment is multisensory so why is it necessary to have a constructed MSE? The short answer is, for able bodied children who can partake in the natural environment in meaningful ways, a constructed MSE is not necessary. The necessity arises when a child cannot partake in the multisensory aspects of the natural environment in meaningful ways. For some children the natural environment seems chaotic and unpredictable. When such a child is left without appropriate environmental modifications, the child's ability to engage with the external environment may be seriously compromised. The child will require an environment which is individually tailored to meet his or her particular needs.

Good teaching involves making matches between the child's ability and the task difficulty. When the child has no problems – that is, has no sensory impairment, achieves age-appropriate developmental milestones, has good general intellectual functioning, has good communication skills, is emotionally stable, has few behaviour problems, is physically healthy and has no learning difficulties – making this match between the child's ability and task difficulty is relatively straightforward. Teachers successfully make these matches in ordinary classrooms all the time. Furthermore, there has been a long history of these matches occurring naturally throughout the child's infancy and childhood, which is why in fact the child has achieved developmentally appropriate milestones. The 'teaching-learning paradigm' is clearly an extension of the relationship with the environment (Polloway *et al.* 2001, p. 19). The child learnt to see by visually engaging with the environment; the infant saw an object and tried to reach it. The child learnt to hear by aurally engaging with the environment; the infant heard a noise and tried to identify it. The child is genetically programmed to learn and develop and engagement with the natural environment strongly helps make it happen.

Somewhere along the ability continuum from normal ability to PMLD there is a cut-off point where the role of the environment changes from simply being an extension of the teaching-learning paradigm to assuming a much more fundamental role. Interaction with the environment plays a powerful role in shaping the child's development and learning. When the child has very little vision, or hearing, very low intellectual functioning, difficulty in perceiving environmental order will affect learning and development. A more user friendly environment that is more constant and predictable for the child is required to facilitate that learning and development.

Unless appropriate changes are made to the environment the child is 'at risk of withdrawing emotionally and physically to the security of... [his or her] own internal sensation' (White and Telec 1998, p. 104). The child may withdraw to an internal world of nonproductive self-engagement – the child ceases to be an active citizen of the world. Learning and development, which is largely dependent upon engagement with the outside world, may be put on hold, or even begin to regress.

For the nondisabled child the role of the environment can almost be taken for granted. This is because the natural non-engineered environment is abundantly rich for each child with normal ability. If environmental engineering is required, the child is generally independently able to effect these changes, thereby ensuring that learning and development continue to occur in spontaneous and natural ways. The child on the other side of this cut-off line is not able to independently achieve this level of environmental engineering. This child is dependent upon others making the environmental changes for him or her. For the child with normal sense ability the one global natural environment is sufficient. In contrast, for the child with PMLD this natural environment is not structured enough to foster development. The child will require an environment which is individually tailored to meet his or her particular needs.

The teaching-learning paradigm can be illustrated using a triangle where the apex represents the one natural environment and the base represents the many individually engineered environments (see Figure 1.2).

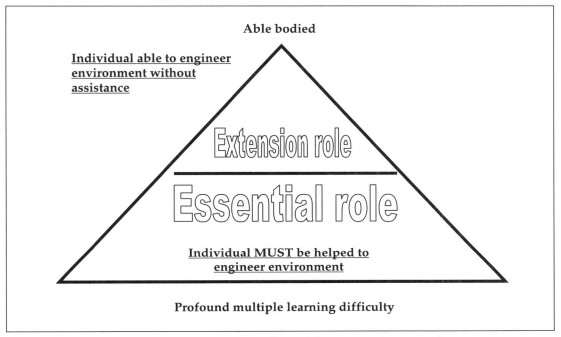

Figure 1.2   Role of the environment in the teaching-learning paradigm

The teaching-learning paradigm is divided into an upper triangle where the environment is an extension of the teaching-learning paradigm and a lower section where the environment plays an essential role. Children are positioned in the upper triangle if they fit into the regular classroom without the need for environmental changes. Children are positioned in the lower part of the triangle when they require special environmental changes to be made. The lower they are positioned on the triangle the greater the number of environmental changes that are required. When the environment is an essential part of the teaching-learning paradigm educators must develop individualised education plans which maximise the programme-environment-individual fit. One achieves this fit through the use of multisensory approaches and/or multisensory environments.

What is a multisensory environment?

A **multisensory environment** is a dedicated space or room:

> ... where stimulation can be controlled, manipulated, intensified, reduced, presented in isolation or combination, packaged for active or passive interaction, and temporally matched to fit the perceived motivation, interests, leisure, relaxation, therapeutic and/or educational needs of the user. It can take a variety of physical, psychological and sociological forms.
>
> (Pagliano 1998, p. 107)

The MSE is built from the child out. The environment is built to fit the needs of the child. Stimulation is fashioned to appeal to the child's sense abilities. For the child with PMLD the relationship between self and the external environment is tenuous. The child's sense windows to the outside world can be so narrow, rigid, inflexible, unstable or fragile that extensive and ongoing environmental engineering is necessary to increase the likelihood of learning and development occurring. Learning and development will only occur if sensory stimulation is meaningful to the child.

Multisensory stimulation

Stimulation is **multisensory** when it appeals to more than one sense modality. We sense the world via the transmission of thousands of sensory receptors. These somatosensory (from Greek *soma* 'body') receptors can be divided into two broad classes: proprioceptors and exteroceptors (see Table 1.1). Together the proprioception and exteroception systems combine to inform the individual where self ends and the environment begins.

Proprioceptors are receptors that receive stimuli that describe the current state of our body. They include the vestibular apparatus, muscle spindles and Golgi tendon organs. Proprioception (from the Latin *proprius* 'own' and *capere* 'to take') refers to the sensations of position, tension and movement of body parts whether stationary or in flux. Currently proprioception is the preferred term in the literature and subsumes the term **kinesthesia** (from the Greek *kinein* 'to move', *aisthesia* 'perception') the awareness of movement.

Exteroceptors are receptors that receive stimuli that relate to the external environment. Exteroceptors help us detect, identify and locate objects in the environment. These senses include taste, smell, touch and the cutaneous senses (pressure, pain and temperature), hearing and vision.

From the somatosensory receptors information is relayed via neurones to the spinal cord to a variety of locations within the brain. Somatosensory systems are complex and there is considerable interactive crossover. Neurologically there is synaptic inhibition and facilitation at every level from somatosensory receptor to the spinal cord to the brain modifying the nature of the perception. This is why a set stimulus can evoke a variety of responses in different individuals, and in the same individual over time.

Sense modality	Related body part	Function	MSE activity examples
Proprioception (kinesthesia)	Muscles, tendons, joints, inner ear	Informs individual about current state of body (position in space, movement)	Ball pool, waterbed
Vestibular	Semicircular canals located in the inner ear	Equilibrium, balance (response to gravity)	Clock-/anticlock-wise spinning ceiling chair
Muscle spindles	Muscle	Sensations of position, tension and movement	Massage with limb extensions and contractions
Golgi tendon organs	Tendons	Responds to changes in muscle force	Pressing a switch
Exteroception	Sensory receptors of the eyes, ears, mouth, nose and skin	Informs individual about the environment	White room MSE experience
Gustatory	Taste buds (mouth)	Taste	Eating, drinking, licking
Olfactory	Nose	Smell	Smelling an aroma
Tactual	Skin, hair	Touch	Lying prone on fur rug, outline child's body with feather duster
Cutaneous senses	Senses of the skin	Pain Pressure Temperature	Careful positioning of body to reduce pain, discomfort Gentle and firm massage Hot and cold packs
Auditory	Ears	Hearing	Listening to music, sounds
Visual	Eyes	Vision	Watching light show, colours, shapes

Table 1.1 Sense modalities, body parts, functions and MSE activity examples

Engineering the environment

Engineering is 'The art or science of making practical application of the knowledge of pure sciences' (*Macquarie Concise Dictionary* 1997). An engineer is someone who skilfully manages such a project, and in this case the project is organising the child's environment for the purpose of providing opportunities to promote the child's learning and development.

Engineering the environment involves choosing the right environmental resource to create an appropriate environmental compensation, adaptation, adjustment or modification to suit the particular needs of a particular child at a particular time. Engineering is informed by expert knowledge from a wide range of relevant disciplines.

- An *environmental resource* is a source of supply, support or aid that comes from the aggregate of conditions, objects and influences that surround us. In order for these resources to be useful they must be shaped in ways that match the child's needs. Environmental resources in the MSE are multisensory. This means they may relate to any of the aforementioned sense modalities. Environmental compensations, adaptations, adjustments and modifications are created from environmental resources in order to fit particular needs.

- An *environmental compensation* is any addition used to make up for a missing sense ability. For example a deaf child might not be able to hear the school bell so a 'visual bell' is created. This visual bell might consist of prominently positioned flashing lights. The visual bell is used at the same time as the auditory bell. This means the deaf child can independently tell when the school bell is ringing. The visual bell therefore becomes an environmental resource.

- An *environmental adaptation* is any change that is made to the environment which enables the child to use what skills he or she already has. For example a staircase could be adapted by adding a ramp. This would enable the child in a wheelchair to independently move from the ground floor to the first floor. Similarly, the ramp also becomes an environmental resource.

- An *environmental adjustment* is any change which improves one's ability to perceive the environment. For example the focus on a pair of binoculars is adjusted to suit one's visual ability, or a person's hearing aids are adjusted to suit his or her hearing ability.

- An *environmental modification* is any change which makes it easier for the person to engage with the environment. For example a child with low vision could modify the environment to make it easier to see by increasing the lighting and/or by moving his or her eyes closer to the object. Modifications involve simplifying the task in some way, such as by reducing the complexity of the situation by removing irrelevant stimuli.

Environmental resources

The range of environmental resources, particularly those in the MSE, is limited only by the individual's imagination and understanding of the needs of individual children. Environmental resources can be organised by type. For example, environmental resources can be organised by the outcome they produce, such as arousal and relaxation (see Table 1.2).

Sense modality	Arousal	Relaxation
Proprioception (kinesthesia)	Short, fast, irregular spin Turn child upside down	Slow, long, rhythmical rock
Vestibular	Fast, irregular spin	Slow swinging
Muscle spindles	Muscle tension	Muscle relaxation
Golgi tendon organs	Sudden, jerky, unpredictable, movement	Calm, gentle, predictable, movement
Exteroception	Disco	White room
Gustatory (taste)	Hot, spicy food	Comfort food, e.g. hot chocolate, mashed potato
Olfactory (smell)	Peppermint Cinnamon	Chamomile Rose
Tactual	Tickling	Patting, stroking
• pain	Present	Absent
• pressure	Vigorous massage	Smooth, soothing massage
• temperature	Cool	Warm
Auditory	Fast, energetic music	Slow, gentle music
Visual	Bright lights	Low lights

Table 1.2   Examples of environmental resources for arousal and relaxation by sense

Another way to organise environmental resources is according to the size of the child's world. The child learns about the world through his or her senses. The size of the child's world grows as the child becomes more aware.

Learning about the world begins with the senses that inform the individual about the internal state of the body, namely proprioception. The child then starts to become aware of the near external world through the cutaneous senses, the tactual sense, the olfactory sense and the gustatory sense.

The two senses that provide opportunities for the child to access the more distant world similarly begin as near sense experiences then gradually expand outwards. It is not until the near visual and auditory skills have been established that the child begins to explore further afield. Cognition is the final common pathway integrating somatosensory stimulation (see Figure 1.3).

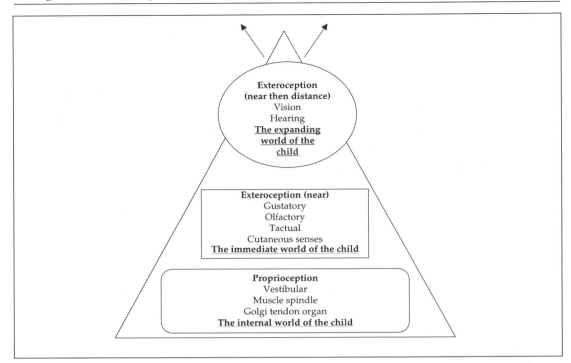

Figure 1.3   The expanding world of the child – cognition is the final common pathway

Children with PMLD may have an extremely small world because they might not have yet mastered the near visual or near auditory skills which would enable them to move on to the next stage of learning about the world. It is therefore most important for the educator to be aware of the size of the child's perceived world and to create environmental experiences that fit inside this world.

Environmental engineering in action

Unless the environment is carefully engineered, the child with a sense impairment will experience difficulty making sense of the world. For example, for a blind infant even a simple, everyday experience like being picked up can be problematic. The sighted infant sees that he or she is about to be picked up and makes the necessary preparations based on previous experiences of being picked up. The blind infant, however, misses out on the visual advance organiser and consequently may find being picked up startling, even unpleasant. Furthermore each experience of being picked up seems different and unrelated.

Caregivers therefore must compensate, by verbally announcing their presence and tactually informing the infant of their intention to pick him or her up. This will help the infant make sense of the experience. If the caregivers consistently provide the same compensations over time, these will help the infant link the current experience of being picked up with previous experiences of being picked up.

When consistent, meaningful compensations are not provided, the infant may begin to resist being picked up. The stronger the infant's resistance the more likely this resistance will result in fewer caregiver-infant interactions and fewer opportunities for the infant to engage with the outside world in purposeful ways. Without the appropriate environmental compensations, lack of vision has the potential to substantially slow down developmental outcomes.

When the child is both deaf and blind the compensations need to come from the other sense modalities. For example, the caregiver could gently touch the child and provide a body sign that would inform the child that he or she was about to be picked up. It is important to remember that if the child is both deaf and blind this will have significant impact on the size of the child's perceived world.

Kick start or catalyst

The larger the number of disabilities and the more profound those disabilities are, the greater the need for highly specialised environmental engineering. Instead of the spontaneous and natural relationship which develops between the able bodied child's learning and the environment, the child with profound multiple learning difficulties requires some kind of 'kick start... or... catalyst' (Porter and Miller 2000, p. 8) to get a particular sense ability working – particularly the visual and auditory senses.

The authors use the words of a teacher of children with PMLD to explain:

> Sometimes children will begin to develop visual skills, which they haven't [used] before because they haven't had that amount of contrast before... A couple of children have made enough progress so that no one would be in any doubt that they had some sight, even though their notes say they are blind... one child was in a wheelchair. He kept his hands under his tray and didn't want to interact... He did begin to get interested in things under the ultraviolet light and did begin to reach and... to reach out to bright things in a normal environment. At the same time he was beginning to walk and use a rolator. Then he had reason to use his light perception because he was beginning to move. So his whole development has been aided by him learning to use his vision in that kind of way... He still needs very high contrast. (p. 8)

Visual stimulation activities in the MSE helped the boy to take more of an active interest in vision and provided the kick start or catalyst for the boy to begin to use his functional vision to help him walk with the aid of a rolator. Hall and Bailey (1989) define *functional vision* as 'the use of vision for purposeful behavior' (p. 390).

The more profound the impairment and the larger the number of learning difficulties the greater the need for educators to carefully consider the relationship between the child and the environment. It is this relationship between the child and the environment which provides the key for the child to make sense of the world, to be able to use those senses that are available to that child for purposeful behaviour.

Functional sense use is the use of a particular sense for purposeful behaviour.

13

How can stimulation be shaped?

Every significant word used in the definition of the MSE will now be defined. These definitions are interwoven with examples which have been based on the following nine stages of skill development in children with PMLD (Kozloff and Rice 1998). They are:

- **preacquisition** – child shows skill readiness but skill not yet acquired;
- **acquisition** – child learns the basic components of a skill;
- **fluency** – child learns to perform the skill accurately and proficiently;
- **endurance** – child able to engage in the skill for an extended period of time;
- **momentum** – child able to engage in the skill despite distractions;
- **generalisation** – child able to transfer or apply skill learnt in one environment or situation to another environment or situation;
- **adaptation** – child adds a modification to make skill more personally relevant;
- **retention** – child retains skill over time. Retention can be applied to acquisition, fluency, endurance, momentum, generalisation and adaptation;
- **maintenance** – child has achieved independence and therefore does not require further instruction regarding this skill.

Control means regulation. The goal is to regulate the stimulus so it is meaningful to the child. For example, a big yellow switch attached to a fan may allow the child to control the fan. Each time the child presses the switch the child receives a refreshing breeze as a reward. If the child finds the experience meaningful then this form of stimulus control will provide an opportunity for the child to learn about the relationship between cause and effect using acquisition (learning how to activate the fan by pressing the switch), fluency (developing accuracy and proficiency with practice) and endurance (keeping the activity going over a period of time).

Manipulation means the skilful or artful management of some process, especially a sense ability, so that it is more suitable to one's purpose or more advantageous to the user. Information obtained during the control phase is used to manipulate the stimulation so that it continues to become even more meaningful for the user. For example, the big yellow switch could be manipulated by adding a ten second timer. The child must now reactivate the switch every ten seconds in order to obtain the breeze reward. The repetition involved in activating the switch provides increased opportunities for the child to learn about the relationship between cause and effect. The management strategy used here is to test the momentum of the child by carefully introducing a distraction, namely a reduction in fan time.

Intensity refers to the degree or extent of energy, strength or force applied. Particular adjectives are used to describe intensity for each sense ability, e.g., a sound can vary in volume from soft to loud, or in pitch from low to high. Once the child achieves proficiency at activating the fan, the activity where the fan runs for ten seconds might begin to lose its interest. It is therefore beneficial to introduce some change to the activity. Having ways to change an activity is important because the more something remains the same, the less noticeable it becomes and hence less stimulating. Children notice what is different. It is the difference which helps the child learn to retain the skill over time. The speed of the fan could be turned from one to two on the dial thereby increasing air flow from light breeze to a slightly stronger breeze. The intensification of the stimulus provides a way to extend the activity and helps the child to continue to learn about the relationship between cause and effect.

Reduction refers to the act of bringing something down in degree or extent, strength or force. Reducing the speed of the fan from forceful wind (say five on the dial) to light breeze (one on the dial) could be just as interesting for the child as increasing the intensity. Further reductions could be obtained by decreasing the timer from ten to five seconds or moving the fan so that it is further away from the child. These new experiences all help to reinforce the connection between cause (activating the switch) and effect (receiving the breeze reward). They also help the child begin to make generalisations.

Educators must be aware of how the stimulation is being presented. Each of the above examples describe situations where the stimulus (the breeze reward) is presented *in isolation*. Even though the stimulus is controlled, manipulated, intensified or reduced there is just one reward. The child activates the switch and receives a single reward, namely a breeze.

Stimulation can also be *combined* with other sense rewards. These rewards can be linked to either same and/or other sense rewards (see Table 1.1). For example, if a second switch was placed beside the first switch with a fan that was located on the other side of the child this would enable the child to make a choice. The child could choose to activate just one fan, or each fan in succession, or both in unison. This choice enabled the child to adapt the activity to suit personal requirements. If the child had not yet reached the stage of adaptation the act of combining stimulation could also be used to test the child's momentum. For example, colourful plastic streamers could be attached to the fan. This would provide the child with a visual reward to accompany the breeze. The activity could be further changed by moving the fan closer to the child so that the streamers gently tickled the child's face or alternatively, a scent spray could be linked to the switch thereby providing the child with an olfactory reward as well as the breeze. Now when the child pressed the switch a spray of orange blossom scent accompanied the breeze and/or the streamers. These activities all help to build on the original experience and when provided in ways that precisely match the child's learning needs help the child learn to make generalisations that can be applied to other situations, such as in the classroom or at home.

How can the needs of the user be identified?

In the previous section we examined ways that stimulation can be shaped and presented. The next step is to identify the needs of the user.

Identifying the needs of the user is perhaps the most difficult task we face. The problem is, where to start? I like to begin by stepping back and considering what are the needs of all human beings. Such a process helps me to gain a more dignified perspective and prevents me from overfocusing on the child's disabilities.

The Canadian philosopher Mark Kingwell (2000) in his book, *The World We Want: Virtue, Vice and the Good Citizen*, lists seven roles. I think these seven roles provide a useful platform from which to begin to identify the needs of children with PMLD. He writes:

> Even a cursory survey of the range of human life would have to conclude that we inhabit, with varying degrees of enthusiasm, at least six roles that are not directly political. Let's consider them for a moment.
>
> We are (1) *inquirers*, seeking the truth about our lives and the universe in which we live. We are (2) *moral agents*, seeking to discern, do, and defend what we consider is the right thing. We are (3) *householders and consumers*, involved in a daily round of dwelling, eating, and entertaining. We are, necessarily, (4) *workers or economic agents*, engaging in the labour that makes dwelling possible. We are (5) *cultural beings*, who enjoy the fruits of human creativity in everything from staged performances and recorded music to the pictures we hang on our walls or the television we watch and books we read. And we are (6) *intimates*, creators of love and emotional connection in our relationships with our friends and families.
>
> ...[and one which is directly political namely, (7)] citizen... (pp. 13-14)

These seven roles relate directly to children with PMLD. In simplified form they are:

(1) *inquirers* – engaging with self, objects, people and events in purposeful ways;
(2) *moral agents* – making choices;
(3) *householders and consumers* – daily living;
(4) *workers or economic agents* – being productive, being active;
(5) *cultural beings* – enjoying human creativity;
(6) *intimates* – creators of love and emotional connections – communication;
(7) *citizens* – being self-determining, influencing and shaping the world in which we live.

These seven roles help us collect information about the child that will be useful and affirming. We know that the child needs his or her senses in order to become an *inquirer*. Therefore we must identify what functional sense abilities the child actually has so that we can begin to expand them.

Interests are those particular things that an individual finds engaging. Educators need to make close observations to find out what the child's personal likes and dislikes are and to use this knowledge when working with the child in the MSE. Using the switch to activate the fan could be one interest but, once the child has learnt to generalise, the child might also like to use the switch to activate a cassette recorder to play favourite music tapes. The child could learn how to choose which activity he or she would like to do. This makes the child a *moral agent*. It also makes the child a *consumer* and a *cultural being*.

Active refers to activities that require the child to be expressive in some way. This means that the child has been productive. The child has produced an action. For example, the child activates the big yellow switch to obtain the breeze reward. If the child does not activate the switch nothing happens, nothing is produced. The fan only starts when the switch is activated by the child, when the child becomes a worker.

Passive refers to activities which involve the child being receptive to the experience but it does not involve any expressive participation. The child is not productive. If someone other than the child pressed the switch connected to the fan then the child would receive the breeze reward without having been actively involved in starting the fan. The activity would therefore be passive. The child simply observes the fan being turned on and then passively enjoys the breeze.

It is important to identify ways to help make passive activities more active. For example, a timer could be used to stop the fan after 20 seconds. This would require the child to communicate that he or she would like the fan to be turned back on. In this way the child begins to be productive, which in turn means that the child is learning how to shape his or her world.

Time is a prescribed or allocated period. It is a particular moment at which something takes place. When working with children with PMLD in the MSE timing is crucial. Many of the examples we have so far considered include a timing component. Activities need to be temporally matched to suit the child's ability to attend. Attention can be divided into three parts: coming to attention, maintaining attention and doing something with the attention. Educators therefore must measure the child's attention as it specifically relates to a particular activity and design the activity to fit the child's ability. For example it might be better to begin the fan activity by providing the child with a substantial reward, say 60 seconds (this would help the child come to attention, to become aware that there is a pleasant breeze). Then once the child begins to better understand the nature of the task (i.e. is able to reactivate the fan in a shorter period of time) the length of the reward might be shortened. This process provides opportunities for the child to begin to shape the world in ways that are meaningful for him or her. The child becomes a *citizen* of the world.

Motivation is the act of providing someone with something which prompts a person to act. Educators who use the MSE must make close observations in order to understand what motivates a particular child. Motivation consists of three components: direction (where the individual chooses to invest his or her energy), intensity (how much energy is invested in the task) and persistence (long term investment). For example, the fan activity might be an excellent activity during summer when the child is hot. We could say the hot summer weather motivates the child to want to activate the switch to turn on the fan. The hot weather might help to provide the child with a direction. The length of time the fan is activated each time the switch is pressed is likely to influence the intensity of the child's involvement. If the fan only runs for one second then the child may decide not to continue with the activity. If the fan runs for 20 seconds then the child may decide the reward is worth the effort involved in activating the switch.

Many children with PMLD experience very low levels of stamina. This means they find it extremely difficult to keep up an activity over the long term. This inability to persist with an activity seriously inhibits learning. The child might acquire a skill but is unable to generalise or internalise the skill because of insufficient practice. The educator therefore needs to work out ways to maximise success.

If the child begins to believe that continuing the activity will lead to greater success then the child is more likely to continue trying. Educators help convince the child that he or she is achieving greater success by identifying personal achievement goal orientations for the child. These may include the child obtaining a highly valued reward, marked improvement in personal performance or increased social recognition for a job well done.

Leisure is free or unrestricted time. Children with PMLD are likely to spend large amounts of time on their own so it is important they learn how to use leisure time constructively.

Recreation is refreshment by means of some pastime or agreeable exercise which affords both relaxation and enjoyment. Activities like learning how to activate a cassette recorder to play music expand the child's repertoire of leisure time options and help make unrestricted time more purposeful and personally satisfying.

Life for children with PMLD can be very stressful. It can be frustrating not being able to communicate effectively. Not having communication skills often means that the child finds it difficult to shape his or her understanding of the world and achieves little success in shaping his or her environment. It can be particularly difficult contending with bodies that do not work properly. Some children tire easily and others are in pain or experience severe discomfort. Children therefore need opportunities for relaxation.

Relaxation is the process of becoming less tense and rigid. The MSE provides a range of activities for relaxation including sensory stimulation, massage and entertainment.

Arousal means to excite into action and can be both physiological and mental. Increased levels of arousal result in a faster heart rate and respiration, muscles that are more tense, higher blood pressure and increased intellectual alertness. An individual's arousal level can therefore be correlated with observations of heart rate, respiration rate and muscle tension. The relationship between arousal and performance is a bell shaped curve. However, peak performance is not just dependent on the level of arousal. Factors such as wellbeing, hunger, thirst, medication and time of day affect the height and width of the curve.

Anxiety is a subjective state which relates to the individual perceiving the environment to be threatening in some way, usually because there is a discrepancy between the demands of a situation and the individual's ability to meet those demands. Children with PMLD often find themselves in anxiety inducing situations. Creating an environment that is less threatening to the child is therefore a fundamental function of the MSE.

Stimuli can be organised to create an environment which is relaxing where the emphasis is on leisure and recreation or they can be used for education and/or therapy.

Education in the MSE is the process where the child develops and learns to use his or her faculties (especially the sense abilities) so that they can be deployed in more purposeful ways.

Therapy is the treatment of a disease, disorder or defect to arrest, minimise deterioration, remediate, cure and/or restore the individual's physical or psychological ability. This treatment may also involve helping the individual learn to adapt to particular problems posed by disability.

Often there is considerable overlap between relaxation, education and therapy. This is particularly important when the child is experiencing high levels of frustration and anxiety. The MSE provides a suitable environment for this overlap to occur seamlessly. For example, the speech language pathologist may teach the child to use a yes/no voice box to choose between a massage on the mattress or a game in the ball pit. If the child chooses the massage the activity might begin with a relaxation activity where the child lies back and watches a projected image slide along the wall in time with gentle music. The teacher may follow this relaxation activity with a massage. Each body part being massaged might be named and associated with basic concepts like 'Massage hand'. After the relaxation activity the physiotherapist may use the time on the mattress to measure joint range leg and arm movements. If the child chooses the ball pit, the occupational therapist may encourage the child to pick up and pass balls to the therapist. Such an activity provides further opportunity for communication and the learning of basic concepts.

What equipment can be used?

Table 1.3 provides a summary of popular items that are currently used in the MSE. This is by no means an exhaustive list. The range of equipment that can be included in the MSE is almost limitless. You can find out more about this equipment through commercial catalogues which can be found on the world wide web. Often equipment can be homemade. This means that the designer can design the equipment to match an individual child's specific needs.

Item	Description	Outcome
Activity-complete switch*	Operates when activity correctly completed.	Keep student engaged in an activity, go on to next activity.
Air cushion/mattress	Variety of sizes, shapes, colours and prices.	Sitting, lying, relaxation.
Aromatherapy diffuser, aroma fan, interactive aroma box, fog smell machine, essential oils, massage oils*	Pomanders, scented pockets, cushions, smell box, incense, essential oils.	Aromatherapy and massage for relaxation, stimulation, exercise, passive activity. Stimulates the olfactory sense.
Ball pools plus soft play frame	Variety of sizes, shapes and prices. Balls clear, white, single or multicoloured. Ball size (diameter 6 to 7.5 cm). Net for washing balls required.	Small balls suit younger children. Larger balls suit larger children and more active use. Provide safety, body support. Clear balls for illumination from under ball pool.
Balls (various sizes, textures), balloons	For physiotherapy, exercise, play, sport.	Exercise, proprioception, hand-eye coordination.
Beanbags	Variety of sizes, shapes, colours and prices.	Sitting, lying, relaxation, good for positioning student in an activity to ensure child can use vision, and hands.
Bubble tube, bubble wall, bubble column mirrors*	Diameter 15 or 30 cm. Length 1 to 1.75m. Boiled/distilled water, change regularly. Bubble speed slow to fast. Switch to control coloured lights or automatic slow colour change.	Visual effect produced by rising bubbles and lighting plus sounds. Gentle vibration makes pleasing tactile effect. Combined visual, auditory and tactile experience.
Ceiling chair, leaf chair	Various designs to cradle body for lying or sitting.	Proprioception.
Crystal pulse amplifier box and microphone*	Attached to solar 250 projector and to sound source.	Visual reward when sounds are made.
Fans, wind generator*	Fan with safety grill can be attached to a switch.	Cause effect, tactile stimulation.
Fibre optics, fountain tails, waterfall, curtain,	Glass fibre encased in a silicone rubber or PVC	Light can be touched, moved, explored

continued

Item	Description	Outcome
spray, wall, carpet, travelling light tube, picture maker, fibre-optic torch (flash light) lamp, light source (colour changer)*	sheath to give protection and flexibility. Light from source extends along the length of the fibre. Fixed or mobile.	manipulated. Changing colours encourage focus of attention. Decoration or cool lighting.
Flood light (with filter pack)*	Creates a pool of light (five colours - yellow, red, green, blue,orange).	Visual stimulation.
General lighting with dimmers*	Natural lighting for the space needed for cleaning and setting up equipment.	To aid movement in, out and within MSE. Relaxation.
Hydrotherapy Jacuzzi/whirlpool, trough, bath, shower, waterfall, fountain, inflatable pool mattress and toys, life vest, water toys*	Full range of water equipment. Water treatment necessary. Water safety requirements.	Hydrotherapy, water play, proprioception, movement, stimulation relaxation.
Mirror ball, multicoloured mirror ball, pin spot, rotator (drive unit), sparkle ball (alternative)*	Diameter 20 to 30 cm. Spotlight shone onto slowly rotating ball to cast myriad of moving light reflections.	Creates interesting visual effects, atmosphere. If located on ceiling lights entire space.
Mirrors of various kinds	Mirrors can be used to magnify effects – with bubble tube, fibre optic spray, helps create atmosphere.	Enable child to view self doing the activity within the MSE.
Musical instruments*	Percussion instruments: drum, tambourine, triangle, bar chimes, cabasa, egg shakers, wrist bells, finger cymbals, maracas, rain pipes, rainmaker, whistles, woodblock, electronic organ.	Auditory stimulation, hand-eye coordination, leisure, recreation.
Plasma ball*	A glass globe that responds to either sound or hand contact to produce visual effect.	Tactile, visual, auditory cause and effect. Suitable for withdrawn user.
Shimmering curtain	Covers entrance so people coming and going do not disturb the ambience of the room.	Prevents interruptions when people come into and leave the MSE.

continued

Item	Description	Outcome
Soft play – floor, walls, ceiling, furnishings, seats, beds, cushioning, solid shapes – sausages, wedges, triangles, semi-circle, circles, rectangles, squares (cubes), tubes, caves, tunnels	Nylon re-inforced flame retardant foam to make a wide range of cushions and shapes. Velcro strips for linking units together.	For movement activities, relaxation and leisure, construction, manipulation, experimentation, social play.
Solar 250 projector. Wheel rotator. Prism/kaleidoscope lens. Variety of wheel effects (6″), silhouette projector*	Slowly-moving fluid patterns or special images are thrown onto the walls, floor and ceiling.	Creates interesting visual effects. Atmosphere. If located on ceiling, lights large space. Can be focused on one wall.
Sound and light floor or wall, hopscotch, sound effects units, microphones, sound sensitive toys*	Sound-activated visual displays. Weight-activated visual and sound displays. Sound-activated visually organised response (e.g. louder for higher).	Tactile, visual and auditory cause and effect.
Soundbeam, Midisynthesiser, Midicreator (similar to soundbeam but less sensitive). Midigesture, midisensor*	Consists of a control box and transducer. A beam bounces back from an object (e.g. hand). The transducer emits an electronic pulse to a particular note or chord – if object moves closer, note becomes higher (MIDI Musical Instrument Digital Interface).	If range is very short, slightest movement will produce sound changes – suit immobile child. Movement and auditory reward. Movement and auditory cause and effect.
Sound system, collection of CDs, cassettes*	CD, cassette player, radio.	For background music, sound effects, stories. Relaxation.
Spotlight and colour wheel*	Constantly rotating sparkles of light. Unit gets hot so attach to ceiling.	Visual stimulation, tracking.
Switches Touch pads (or pressure pads), large (125cm diameter), small (30mm	Switches can be brightly coloured and come is a variety of different	User control, self-determination, cause and effect, perseverance.

continued

Item	Description	Outcome
diameter), for feet, hands, squeeze, lever, collar, head tilt switch – controller device*	shapes. Can be designed to be operated by head/hand/feet or other body part movement.	
Switches - Remote control*	Operated from a distance.	Able to activate TV, CD player, air conditioning.
Switches - Sensor proximity switches*	Activates when a person approaches the switch.	User control.
Tactile panels, walls, features, carpets, hangings, koosh balls	Different textures to provide a variety of tactile sensations. Can be made out of household items such as broom and mop heads, brushes, plastic plates, string, wool.	Tactual stimulation, exploration.
Television set with VCR, collection of video material*	Television monitor to show videos.	For entertainment, visual and auditory stimulation, interest, create atmosphere, relaxation.
Tents (white net)	Brings projected image closer to viewer. Can be placed over waterbed.	Visual stimulation, makes space smaller, more private.
Ultraviolet effects (UV type A light), fluorescent hoops, rods, paint, pens. Markers, balls, globes (earth, moon, planets), galaxy. Linelite plastic tubing, magic wands*	For use in dark room. Some effects depend upon UV lamp. Some effects use normal white light.	Highly stimulating visually. Visual exploration. Draw pictures. Write 'glow in the dark' messages.
Water beds, water bed plinths, vibroacoustic water bed (person feels the music)*, variety of covers (fur, velvet, cotton)	Variety of sizes, types, colours and prices. Requires strong floor support.	Adjusts to body weight. For comfort and relaxation. Tactual, proprioception.
Wind chimes, mobiles	Wind chimes of any shape or size. Mobiles of any shape or size. Can be activated by wind, or by movement of the child, directly or by attached string.	Auditory stimulation. Visual stimulation. Hand-eye coordination. Cause effect.

*Power connection required (battery or electricity)

Table 1.3 Items that could be included in a MSE

What are the principal MSE design prototypes?

The physical, psychological and sociological forms of the MSE encompass 12 design prototypes, each with a particular design feature (Pagliano 2000). They are: the white room, the grey room, the dark room, the sound space, the interactive area, the water area, soft play, the portable environment, the virtual environment, the inclusive area, the pluralist environment and the social space.

1. The white room

Most people equate the white room with the 'snoezelen' (although the original snoezelen consisted of a series of different rooms not just a white room). The white room (see Table 1.4) is the most common MSE prototype and it is most often used by children with PMLD. It is principally for relaxation although other uses are possible. All prototypes are 'open-minded' spaces and therefore are potentially multifunctional in design. The white room consists of white ceiling, walls and floor to form a giant 3D screen on which visual effects can be projected by a wheel effects projector and/or a pin spot focused on a rotating mirror ball. An alternative is to use off-white or even pastel colours rather than white for ceiling, walls and floors. Popular white room equipment include a light show, sound system, bubble tubes, a ball pit, water bed, mattress and a fibre optic spray. As with each prototype the range of possible equipment that can be included is limited only by the imagination of the designers.

Function	Description	Equipment
Leisure, recreation, relaxation	White ceiling, walls, floor provide a 3D screen to present visual effects in isolation or in combination with other visual effects and/or non-visual effects. *Neutral ground (white) with (visual/non-visual) figure.*	General lighting with dimmers, mirror ball and rotator, pin spot, projector plus wheel rotator, prism kaleidoscope lens, wheel effects, colour wheel, bubble tube, water bed, bean bag, mattress, cushions, wind chime, sound equipment, mobiles, tactile wall panels, ball pool, ceiling chair, fibre optic spray.

Table 1.4   MSE design prototype 'The white room'

2. The grey room

Philip (2000) reported on a classroom for children with foetal alcohol syndrome which was specifically designed to reduce stimulus. The grey room (see Table 1.5) is soundproofed, with grey ceiling, walls and grey carpeted floor. Grey curtains obscure windows and grey dust-covers hide equipment and materials not currently in use. These measures reduce or eliminate extraneous stimulus and help prevent the child from being distracted.

The room is specifically designed for children who experience problems in the three facets of attention: coming to attention, maintaining attention and doing something with their attention. Single stimulus effects are therefore presented within a context of minimum distraction. Children wear a weighted vest, which gives them an increased sense of place. The room has lines on the floor to indicate set places for set activities. When being with other children becomes too difficult a child may retreat to an enclosed, miniature, grey carpet covered, cushioned den located at the back of the room. When participating in class activities children sit on a small square of carpet or at a carrel, a high walled, three sided desk which reduces distraction and supports independent work.

Function	Description	Equipment
Stimulus reduction	Soundproofed room consisting of grey ceiling, walls, and grey carpeted floor constructed to provide a consistently dull background to ensure minimum distractions, particularly those of a visual or auditory nature. *Single effect (figure) presented within a context (ground) of minimum distraction.*	Grey curtains cover windows, grey dust-covers hide equipment and materials currently not in use, weighted vest gives child a sense of place as do lines drawn on the classroom floor; a miniature grey carpet covered, cushioned den provides a calming retreat for time out (Philip 2000); a carrel provides a private workstation where a child can work without being interrupted.

Table 1.5   MSE design prototype 'The grey room'

3. The dark room

The dark room (see Table 1.6), with its black ceiling, walls and floor forms a giant black ground on which images can be presented with maximum definition and minimum visual distraction. The principal use of the room is for visual stimulation, both ophthalmic and cortical. Supplementary equipment that can be used include spot lights and colour slides, fibre-optic spray, iridescent paint and play dough, coloured and ultraviolet lights, and pen light torches (flash lights).

Function	Description	Equipment
Visual stimulation	Black ceiling, walls, and floor provide black environment for maximum definition of visual effect (figure) with minimum visual distraction. *Visual ground minimised (black) with visual figure intensified. Figure ground relationship adjusted to suit visual skills, interests and abilities.*	Spot lights with colour slides, fibre-optic spray, iridescent paint, play dough, coloured lights, ultravoilet light, pen light torches (flash lights), fluorescent hoops, rods (glow tubes).

Table 1.6   MSE design prototype 'The dark room'

4. The sound space

The sound space (see Table 1.7) is a soundproofed room enclosed by wooden ceiling, walls and sprung wooden floor. Soundproofing ensures that the space is not contaminated by extraneous noises. The room can be organised to be acoustically sharp or dull. Sounds can be presented in isolation or in combination, produced by self or by others. The goal is to minimise the auditory ground while intensifying the auditory figure. The facilitator adjusts the figure ground relationship to suit the child's auditory skills, interests and abilities.

Function	Description	Equipment
Auditory stimulation	Soundproofed room made of wooden ceiling, walls and sprung wooden floor, provides acoustically sharp or dull environment for listening to sounds, in isolation or combination, produced by self or others, in purest form possible. *Auditory ground minimised (soundproofing) with auditory figure intensified. Figure ground relationship adjusted to suit auditory skills, interests and abilities.*	Resonance board for child to lie on and listen to self-produced sounds both vocal and/or percussive (Nielsen 1994). Musical instruments for child to listen to or play. Percussion instruments: drum, tambourine, wood blocks, gong, triangle, whistle, clappers. Switch activated horn. Electric organ Tape/CD/radio, headphones, FM, microphone, amplifier, sound beam, echo chamber.

Table 1.7   MSE design prototype 'The sound space'

The principal use of the sound space is auditory stimulation, therefore it would suit those with hearing impairment, both auricular and cortical. Equipment might include a resonance board for the child to lie on and listen to self-produced vocal or percussive sounds (Nielsen 1994) and musical instruments for the child to listen to or play (percussion instruments: drum, tambourine, wood blocks, gong, triangle, whistle, clappers, switch activated horn, electric organ), tape/CD/radio, headphones, FM, microphone, amplifier, sound beam and echo chamber.

5. The interactive area

The interactive area (see Table 1.8) is a place where vocal or movement sensitive switches enable a child to consistently and immediately produce an effect that is rewarding and meaningful for the child. The principal use of this area is to promote an understanding of the relationship between cause and effect through the use of switches. Switches are designed to suit the ability of individual children. They include large or small touch pads that can be manipulated by toes, feet, fingers, hands, arms, or legs. Manipulation may range from gentle touch to squeeze, they may involve the use of levers, collar switches, even remote control. Multisensory rewards are determined by the imagination of the facilitator: tactile – fans; auditory – music; visual – lights; smell – aroma; taste – food, drink; and interactive – computer games.

Function	Description	Equipment
Understand cause and effect	Equipment, particularly switches, which enable child, by way of small stimulus (vocal or movement) to consistently produce a grand, rewarding response. *Explore relationship between cause and effect.*	Switches designed to suit the ability of individual child – touch pads, large, small, feet, hands, squeeze, lever, collar switch, remote control – multisensory rewards, tactile – fans; auditory – music; visual – lights; smell – aroma; taste – food, drink; interactive – computer games.

Table 1.8   MSE design prototype 'The interactive area'

6. The water area

The water area (see Table 1.9) consists of a pool filled with water. The water area is used for proprioceptive stimulation both static and dynamic. The water (the ground) provides a support for the child's body (figure), and frees the child to move in ways not normally possible outside the water (figure ground relationship). Moving in water is good exercise and helps the child develop body concept, image and awareness. Supplementary equipment such as a jacuzzi, shower, waterfall, slide, lights and heating increases the range of stimulation/activity choices that can be provided.

Function	Description	Equipment
Proprio-ceptive stimulation	Water filled pool plus supplementary equipment. The water supports the child's body, enables child to move in ways not normally possible outside the water. *Personal movement (figure) within a supportive ground (water).*	Water filled pool, jacuzzi, whirlpool, trough, bath, shower, waterfall, fountain, slide, lights, water heating equipment, blow up beach ball, pool toys, inflatable floating mattress.

Table 1.9   MSE design prototype 'The water area'

7. Soft play

The soft play environment (see Table 1.10) is an enclosed space with padded ceiling, and walls. The floor plan may consist of a multi-level set of platforms connected by steps, ramps and wedges made from nylon re-inforced, flame retardant, lead free, PVC filled with fire resistant foam rubber and held in place with velcro strips. The room may also contain large, soft, solid shapes (cubes, pyramids, cones, tubes) made from the same materials as the floor for large scale construction. Additional equipment may include hard plastic moulded shapes to form building blocks and playground equipment, a ball pool, an innersprung mattress or a trampoline. Children use the space to explore, interact with equipment and each other, construct, manipulate objects, experiment, climb, jump, roll, slide, crawl and hide. The soft play environment is a safe place where children can take risks without fear of getting hurt. It is particularly suitable for young children with vision impairment or those with physical disability who are reluctant to play in a regular, less forgiving playground. By creating a safe, secure environment (ground) the child is able to take risks (figure) without the fear of getting hurt (figure ground relationship).

Function	Description	Equipment
Risk taking within a safe space	A soft, enclosed space with padded ceiling and walls, with multi-level floor connected by steps and ramps, where children can explore, take risks, interact with equipment and each other, construct, manipulate objects, experiment. *By creating a safe, secure environment (ground) the child is able to take risks (figure) without the fear of getting hurt (figure ground relationship).*	Cushions, soft solid shapes (cubes, pyramids, cones), steps, ramp, tunnel, wedges and furnishings made from nylon re-inforced, flame retardant, lead free, PVC filled with fire resistant foam rubber with velcro strips for linking. May also include hard plastic moulded shapes, *building blocks playground* equipment, slide, cubby, innersprung mattress, trampoline, ball pool.

Table 1.10   MSE design prototype 'Soft play'

8. The portable environment

The portable environment (see Table 1.11) is a small environment (approximately one to two metres square) that can be folded up and stored in a container for easy transportation from one location to another. A simple example of a portable MSE is a lambswool skin. The lambswool skin might be moved from the cot to the pram to the floor thereby ensuring constancy when the baby first starts to explore environments other than the cot, so in effect it is a transportable comfort zone. The portable environment may be built on a strong cloth base with multisensory features attached using velcro. This means items can be easily removed for cleaning and ensures that they are kept in a stable location in relation to the child. The portable MSE may include a range of multisensory stimulation features (visual, auditory, olfactory), graded in complexity from very simple to challenging. The advantage of this design prototype is that it can be made accessible to children who live in isolated and remote areas. The portable environment is suitable for children of all ages and for home use by parents or caregivers. They can be loaned from toy libraries and resource centres.

Function	Description	Equipment
Easy access for children in isolated areas, home use. Transportable comfort zone	A small environment (approximately 1 to 2 metres square) that can be folded up and stored in a container for easy transportation. May contain a wide range of multisensory stimulation features. *Able to be easily stored and transported.*	Strong cloth base with multisensory features attached using velcro. Items can be easily cleaned and kept hygienic. May follow a theme. May provide a series of sequenced activities gradually increasing in complexity.

Table 1.11 MSE design prototype 'The portable environment'

9. The virtual environment

The virtual environment (see Table 1.12) is achieved through 3D interactive computer imaging. Lanier (1999) identifies the objective of virtual reality as to 'provide exactly the stimulus to the person's sense organs that... [the person] would receive if... [that individual was] in fact in an alternate environment'. For the eyes there are head-mounted displays. For the hands there are gloves which become virtual hands. 'The goal is to see how can you use technology and mould it to a person instead of asking the person to come to the technology... in the future virtual reality systems will be individualized ...' (ibid). Fruchterman (1999) believes advances in computer technology 'will create a world where the individual will have extensive control over his or her personal environment... We are increasingly crossing into an era where technology will be able to accomplish almost anything we can imagine'.

Function	Description	Equipment
For experiences not normally possible in the real world	An environment achieved through 3D interactive computer imaging 'To provide exactly the stimulus to the person's sense organs that... [the person] would receive if... [that individual was] in fact in an alternate environment' (Lanier 1999). *Simulation of real world or imaginary experiences.*	Computer technology programs using monitors – for the eyes there are head mounted displays, for the hand there are gloves which become virtual hands. 'The goal is to see how can you use technology to mould to a person instead of asking the person to come to the technology' (Lanier 1999)

Table 1.12   MSE design prototype 'The virtual environment'

10. The inclusive area

The inclusive area (see Table 1.13) is a normal environment, such as a verandah, garden or playground, converted into an MSE by adding carefully selected, appropriate multisensory features. The result is a space more suitable for those with disabilities, but strongly appealing to all children. The principal use of this design prototype is to promote inclusion in the mainstream. If mainstream schools admit students with disabilities they have a legal responsibility to ensure that the school environment is inclusive, i.e. able to be used by the child with that particular disability in ways that are similar or are parallel to those uses made by nondisabled children.

Function	Description	Equipment
Being with nondisabled peers.	A normal environment, such as a verandah, garden or playground, converted into an MSE by adding carefully selected, appropriate multisensory features. *Making the environment more inclusive, both physically and functionally, by attending to multisensory design features.*	Whatever makes the environment more suitable for children with disabilities – physically suitable e.g., ramps to make it more wheelchair accessible, functional – colours to make parts more easily visible, auditory and tactile features which make it meaningful and safe for blind children to use.

Table 1.13   MSE design prototype 'The inclusive area'

30

11. The pluralist environment

The pluralist environment (see Table 1.14) promotes awareness and a multi-perspective understanding. It focuses on temporal change of the MSE. If the MSE stays the same it becomes stale and both children and staff lose interest. Children notice that which is different. Ideas to help make changes in the MSE can relate to the use of themes (such as the sea, space, festivals, indigenous culture) and performances (such as art exhibitions, music, acting out a story) with value placed on diversity.

Function	Description	Equipment
To embrace diversity	This is an environment where diversity is valued. If the MSE stays the same it becomes stale and children stop participating. Children notice difference if it is presented in a way that matches their ability. *Breathing new life into the built environment by attending to the constancy-change relationship.*	Difference is achieved in many ways: themes (such as the sea, space), festivals, indigenous culture, other cultures, performances (art exhibitions, music, acting out a story).

Table 1.14 MSE design prototype 'The pluralist environment'

12. The social space

The social space (see Table 1.15) helps the child develop a sense of 'who am I?', an essential prerequisite for communication and social interaction. Communication begins with being aware of self, one's needs, wants and desires, being aware of others and wanting to share ideas, experiences or feelings with them. It is a space for special occasions and get togethers. The principal use of this area is to promote a sense of self through communication in a sympathetic environment. This design prototype is different to the other prototypes because it is focuses on social group interaction with peers, whereas the other prototypes focus on individualised, multisensory spaces.

Function	Description	Equipment
To develop social skills	A space for special occasions and get togethers, owned by the children - it's their space. 'If parents and nondisabled brothers and sisters' and friends 'see the children happy, laughing and relaxed, as they so often are in the	Communication dictionary. Speech, sign, augmentative and alternative communication systems. Object-people engagement. Objects. People: peers, family, transdisciplinary team

continued

Function	Description	Equipment
	MSE they're going to relate to them more than if they see them cranky, throwing their arms and legs around, dribbling and angry' (Pagliano 1999, p. 10). *Focus on the social components of an environment.*	members, teachers, therapists, parents, caregivers, psychologists, social workers, teacher's aide, nurses, other.

Table 1.15   MSE design prototype 'The social space'

How does the MSE work in practice?

The hybrid MSE (see Figure 1.4) represents the MSE in its most developed form. It contains features from two or more design prototypes. As stated previously, each design prototype is in itself an 'open-minded' MSE. The hybrid MSE therefore is an eclectic synthesis of the design prototypes. Design prototypes can be combined in different permutations to achieve an infinite number of tailor–made individualised MSEs.

The principal function of the hybrid MSE is to provide a vehicle by which educators can selectively integrate the functions identified in the 12 design prototypes. In the hybrid MSE, team members constantly (re)design the environment to suit the emerging, particular, multiple learning needs, interests and abilities of users. The hybrid MSE therefore is highly flexible and in a continual state of (re)construction (see Table 1.16).

1. The white room --------------->	
2. The grey room --------------->	
3. The dark room --------------->	THE
4. The sound space --------------->	HYBRID
5. The interactive room --------------->	MSE
6. The water area --------------->	CONSISTS OF
7. Soft play --------------->	TWO OR MORE
8. The portable environment --------------->	PROTOTYPE
9. The virtual environment --------------->	DESIGN
10. The inclusive area --------------->	FEATURES
11. The pluralist environment --------------->	
12. The social space --------------->	

Figure 1.4   The hybrid MSE

For example the hybrid MSE might consist of a basic white room setup. The same room might contain a section for visual stimulation that could be closed off with black curtains. The room might be sound proofed and contain a number of features specifically for auditory stimulation. There might be a store room attached to the MSE where a range of equipment such as resonance boards and musical instruments could be kept. There might also be a range of soft play materials. The hybrid MSE is therefore designed to maximise design flexibility so that each educator working in the MSE can redesign the space to fit the precise individual needs of the children in their session.

Function	Description	Equipment
To provide a vehicle by which to selectively integrate the design functions identified in the 12 design prototypes.	An environment which contains two or more features from the 12 design prototypes. *A synthesis of the 12 prototypes enables transdisciplinary MSE team members to construct environments which match the ongoing and changing needs of individual children.*	Endlessly flexible use of equipment – whatever the designers want the space to contain. MSE team members constantly (re)design the hybrid MSE to suit emerging, particular, multiple learning needs, interests and abilities of users.

Table 1.16   The hybrid MSE

Summary

The MSE can be traced back to three developments that occurred in the 1970s – the discotheque, soft play and improved services for people with disabilities. The 'snoezelen' combined the visual and aural ambience of the discotheque with soft play furnishings to create an MSE where individuals with disabilities were in charge. The 'snoezelen', a single function space primarily for relaxation, was replaced by the MSE, a multifunctional 'open-minded' space which could be used for therapy and education as well as for recreation.

Usually learning and development is a spontaneous and natural process of interacting with the environment, that is, unless the child has a disability. The impact of the disability may compromise the child's ability to make sense of the world. Therefore to foster learning and development, the child's environment may be required to be controlled. The number and types of environmental engineering necessary will be primarily determined by the types and severity of the disabilities concerned.

An environmental resource is a source of supply, support or aid that comes from the aggregate of conditions, things and influences that surround us. In order for these resources to be useful, when working with children with PMLD, it is necessary to shape the resources in ways that match the child's needs. Two valuable ways to organise these resources are by outcome (such as arousal and relaxation) or by the size of the child's world, which is determined by the child's sense ability.

Good teaching involves making matches between a child's ability and the task difficulty. When this match occurs naturally, the environment is a simple extension of the teaching-learning paradigm. Such a child does not need an MSE. For children with PMLD however, the environment assumes a much more fundamental role where the use of multisensory approaches and/or MSEs are required.

An MSE is any environment where stimulation of a multisensory nature is precisely engineered to match more closely the exceptional needs of the user. Stimulus may be controlled, manipulated, reduced, presented in isolation or combination, in passive or active forms and modified to suit the child's interests and motivation. Activities may be for recreation, therapy or education.

Nine stages of skill development in children with PMLD are: preacquisition, acquisition, fluency, endurance, momentum, generalisation, adaptation, retention and maintenance. Important social roles for everyone, including children with PMLD, include being an inquirer, making choices, daily living, being active and productive, enjoying human creativity, communicating and making emotional connections, and helping to shape the world in which we live. This philosophy underpins work in the MSE.

There is currently a wide range of equipment on the market that can be used in the MSE. Unfortunately a lot of this equipment is very expensive. Educators are therefore encouraged to also consider designing and making their own equipment.

Twelve design prototypes have been developed, each with a specialist function. The physical forms of the MSE include: the white room (relaxation); the grey room (stimulus reduction); the dark room (visual stimulation); the sound space (auditory stimulation); the interactive area (cause and effect); the water area (proprioceptive stimulation); the soft play environment (risk and safety); the portable environment (transportable comfort zone or activity centre), and the virtual environment (for experiences not normally possible for individuals with a disability). Psychosocial forms include the inclusive area (for environments that facilitate the child with a disability being included with nondisabled children); the pluralist environment (to embrace diversity), and the social space (to develop social skills).

The hybrid MSE comprises a synthesis of two or more features of the 12 design prototypes. The hybrid MSE is therefore designed to maximise design flexibility so that each educator working in the MSE can redesign the space to fit the precise individual needs of the children in their session.

2 Assessment in the MSE

Finding out about the child

Assessing abilities in a child with PMLD is different from assessing abilities in a nondisabled child. Children with PMLD have incompletely developed sensorimotor and cognitive systems and resultant impaired communication. This means that the types of assessment tools and approaches used to assess nondisabled children will not provide sufficiently meaningful or detailed information to be of much assistance when designing an MSE.

Nondisabled children are adaptable. They quickly adjust to new situations and new people. This means they are able to be assessed by adults who do not personally know them. Furthermore the assessors are able to use assessment instruments to collect the information in one sitting.

Children with PMLD experience difficulty adapting to new situations. They find it hard to respond to the requests of someone they do not know or understand. This is further compounded when the child has very limited communication skills anyway. A person who does not know the child possibly will not even recognise that the child is trying to communicate, let alone understand what the child is trying to say. Assessment of the child with PMLD therefore requires that the assessor is well acquainted with the child. The process is slow. Information about the child will need to be collected in small amounts over long periods of time.

The more disabled the child is, the more likely it is that the assessor will need to use finely developed personal skills of observation rather than simply rely on assessment instruments. When assessing nondisabled children, an assessor generally uses an assessment instrument that has been standardised on a large population of children. Such an instrument is valid and reliable for children that statistically fall within two standard deviations from the mean of the general population. Therefore for most children this instrument yields useful assessment information. The assessor need have no particular skills other than having been trained to use the tool to measure the information. Children with PMLD are a small subset of the general population falling well outside the normal range, by definition six standard deviations from the general population mean. There is no standardised, valid, reliable assessment instrument that can be universally applied. Each child is going to have a different set of skills and abilities depending on the nature of the PMLD. Consequently the assessors will need to rely much more heavily on personal expertise regarding how to look and what to look for. The assessors must have exceptional skills of observation and interpretation and these skills will only come from having an indepth understanding of the area through research literature and through extensive practice in this form of assessment.

Therefore when the child with PMLD is taken to specialists for short formal educational assessment using assessment instruments this information will be at best general and not particularly meaningful. This is because the assessment is being conducted out of the child's context by people who do not know the child. The most likely people to be able to obtain meaningful and useful information about the child are going to be the educators who work with the child on a day to day basis and the child's parents or caregivers. Furthermore the most relevant information is likely to be information collected in the actual environment that is familiar to the child.

The MSE is a manipulable environment and when familiar is particularly suited to the conduct of assessment. As one therapist explains:

> We have a very unusual population of children. We would like other people to see our children at their best – especially because the children are difficult to communicate with. If parents and non-disabled brothers and sisters [and friends] see the children happy, laughing and relaxed, as they so often are in the… [MSE], they're going to relate to them more than if they see them cranky, throwing their arms and legs around, dribbling and angry. Unfortunately that's the way they usually are when they see them in the outside world.
>
> (Pagliano 1999, p. 10)

Designing the MSE therefore must be a continuous, ongoing process. The hybrid MSE is organised to maximise design flexibility so that it can be continually redesigned in ways that acknowledge each new piece of assessment information about the child.

Why do we need to find out about the child?

Assessment enables us to conduct a comprehensive audit of the child's current abilities and circumstance. In the past there have been serious problems associated with children with PMLD not receiving proper assessment. Consequently some children may have had correctable sense disabilities which were neither acknowledged nor attended to. For example, a child may have correctable vision loss but has not been prescribed spectacles, or have correctable hearing loss but has not been prescribed hearing aids. The school has a responsibility to be well informed about the sense ability status of each child with PMLD and to ensure that corrective prosthetics are prescribed and used.

Assessment provides an overview of the whole child. It provides evidence of the child's current level of attainment and particular strengths, interests and preferences. Assessment helps us identify which specialists (see Chapter 4) and equipment will be required to work with the child to target the next level of attainment. Assessment and programme development go hand in hand. By identifying the child's current status the child's learning needs become evident. Information obtained from assessment helps us choose instructional strategies that capitalise on what the child already knows. Assessment provides a baseline, a starting point from which to measure whether those instructional strategies have been successful. This is a prerequisite for developing individualised learning outcomes.

What is involved in conducting assessment for the MSE?

Measuring the ability of a child with a severe impairment is complex and challenging. Objective precision is often not possible. Assessment is usually based not on formal tests but on observations and analysis of individual performance. While such assessment may not be objective as in formal testing, it is richly descriptive and qualitative. Assessment is inherently bound to characteristics of the assessor or assessors, unlike in formal testing.

The impairment is not necessarily stable. It can deteriorate (due to disease) or improve (due to treatment or prosthetics). Abilities fluctuate day to day depending on such factors as personal health, medication, and whether or not the child is tired. It is therefore vitally important that assessment is continuous and good records are kept and maintained.

Neisworth and Bagnato (1988) identified eight types of assessment measures. Each of these measures is useful in the MSE. I have therefore used them to develop a particular type of assessment style for use in the MSE.

- *Ecological assessment* focuses on the child's physical, social, physiological development within a range of different environments, not just in the MSE, but also in school, and at home. This assessment often begins with the parents/caregivers questionnaire. It also involves reading through the school file and interviewing significant others in the child's life.
- *Judgement based assessment* involves judgments being made by several MSE team members, each from different disciplines. They make judgements about the child's abilities and skills in a range of different settings. The MSE team is particularly interested in finding out about the child's sense windows to the world. These need to be carefully described.
- *Process assessment* involves elucidating the applicability of various processes used in the MSE for an individual child. For some children who have very low communication skills, assessment might be made by noting and interpreting tiny changes, such as eye movement, less thrashing or less screaming.
- *Interactive assessment* is particularly relevant for the MSE. The evaluation focuses on the reciprocal nature of child-adult interactions, particularly on their content and quality. It is an important form of assessment when looking at the way the child engages with objects, people and events. It therefore helps inform the development of the communication programme.
- *Adaptive-to-handicap assessment* involves modifying content to permit an alternative sensory or response mode. This form of assessment helps the MSE team identify how well an environmental modification (e.g., particular environment or piece of equipment) is matched to the child's needs.

- *Curriculum based assessment* looks at mastery of objectives within a continuum of objectives. It is the major method used in mainstream education and has become increasingly more important in the education of children with PMLD. It is regarded as the key to accountability in education. In the MSE the curriculum will need to be carefully built on assessment information obtained from the ecological assessment, judgement based assessment, process assessment, interactive assessment and adaptive-to-handicap assessment.
- *Norm based assessment* looks at the child's developmental skills compared to the normative group. This form of assessment is useful with children with PMLD in the MSE because it helps ensure that the curriculum is both age- and level-appropriate and incorporates depth, breadth and balance in the way it is devised.
- *Systematic observation* is an essential part of all MSE assessment. It must form the basis of every assessment procedure with children with PMLD. It involves direct observation and the recording of behaviour. This can be through the use of checklists, descriptive notes or video recording. The advantage of using video tape for assessment is that the assessment does not interrupt the proceedings and provides opportunities for the MSE team to work together and to review their observations. The video recording can provide a useful baseline which can be used to show changes in the child over time and can even be used to prepare a report for parents and caregivers.

A ninth form of testing is called *play based assessment*. This is when the student is observed at play and observations are made using play based protocols such as the ones devised by Linder (1990). In play based assessment the emphasis is on the child being in control and the adult merely a facilitator. This fits well with the ethos of the MSE. It is the child that makes the rules and it is the adults' responsibility to ensure that they provide guidance that is built on a well established, mutually trusting and respectful relationship with the child. Play therefore also needs to be an ongoing theme in the way MSE team members develop their assessment protocol. In summary, essentially what I am saying here is that all nine forms of assessment measures need to be woven together to form a specialised form of assessment for use in the MSE. The rest of this chapter will be devoted to showing how this works in practice.

Gathering information systematically

As soon as members of the MSE team start to work with a child they begin to collect information about that child. They use this information to build on what was provided during the parents/caregivers interview. Educators focus on identifying the child's current abilities – particularly those that relate to the MSE. This information is used to inform MSE design and programme development. It is important to avoid listing the child's deficits because such a list does not positively inform programme development nor does it help with MSE design.

Children become inquirers by engaging with themselves, objects, other people and events in purposeful ways. We therefore need to find out as much as we can about the child's abilities to engage with their internal world, their external world and the crossover between the two.

Core assessment areas

Assessment for the MSE has been divided into three core areas. The first area is the parents/caregivers interview and questionnaire. General and specific information about the child is sought. Parents/caregivers are likely to have the best knowledge about the child. They also are a bridge between home, the school and the MSE and can provide a rich contribution to MSE design, development and use.

The second area is functional sense assessment. For the child with PMLD the relationship between self and the external environment is tenuous. Sense windows to the external world can be so narrow, rigid, inflexible, unstable and/or fragile that extensive and ongoing environmental engineering is necessary to facilitate learning and development. Constructing such an environment is therefore dependent on having a comprehensive and accurate understanding of the child's sense windows.

The third area is engagement and communication. The goal of the MSE is to strengthen the child's tenuous sense windows to the outside world thereby increasing the amount of purposeful behaviour through achieving increasingly meaningful engagement with objects, people and events.

The parents/caregivers questionnaire

When you start collecting information about the child it is always best to begin with the parents/caregivers. Parents/caregivers are the people who are likely to know most about their child. The interview helps to delineate the social context of the child. Furthermore, the parents/caregivers interview not only provides you with information about the child, it helps the parents/caregivers to clarify their own ideas about their child and it provides you with a not to be missed opportunity to establish a good working relationship with the child's family. For those who have incorporated MSE type facilities in their own homes there are further opportunities for the MSE team to work closely with the child's family (see Chapter One).

To conduct the parents/caregivers interview:

- Invite parents/caregivers to participate in interview.
- Arrange mutually suitable meeting date/location/time start/finish (e.g. 30 minutes).
- Give parents/caregivers a copy of MSE information sheet beforehand (see Appendix 1).
- Give parents/caregivers copy of the questionnaire beforehand (see Appendix 2).

Contributions from the parents/caregivers need to be actively sought and welcomed so it is a good idea to allow parents at least two weeks to think about the contents of the questionnaire before conducting the interview. The semi-structured, open-ended question interview technique used on the form was chosen to allow the parents/caregivers increased freedom of expression. It is important parents/caregivers understand that the interview and questionnaire are to provide information which will be used to inform MSE design and construction.

In the parents/caregivers questionnaire and interview certain information is sought: firstly social details, then a brief biography and review of the child's current attainment. Next the parents/caregivers assess the child's personality, temperament, interests, likes and dislikes. Lastly the parents/caregivers are encouraged to voice hopes, concerns and fears for both the short-term and long-term. The questionnaire gives insight, not only into the child but also into the parents'/caregivers' attitudes to their child.

At the interview make certain parents/caregivers:

- understand why the interview is being conducted;
- understand what an MSE is (discuss the MSE and answer any questions they might have).

Then the interviewer needs to explain to parents/caregivers:

- that they are being invited to join the MSE team;
- what MSE team membership entails (equal, ongoing access to all information about the child, collective responsibility for MSE programmes and outcomes);
- that parents/caregivers are free to come to school and read through their child's file whenever they wish.

When the interview has been completed write up your report and invite the parents/caregivers to check it to ensure it is accurate. This also provides the parents/caregivers with an opportunity to add any further information they may think is relevant. When the parents/caregivers are happy with the report, confirm permission is given to share the report with other MSE team members.

Personality, interests and temperament

Personality is the assemblage of qualities that make up an individual, the sum total of that person's beliefs, perceptions, emotions and attitudes. Personality includes the mental, emotional and social characteristics of a person. Personality in the Myers-Briggs Type Indicator (Myers and McCaulley 1998) is reduced to four polar scales. They are:

Extroversion .... Introversion

Sensing .... Intuition

Thinking .... Feeling

Judging .... Perceiving

Children with PMLD can be similarly shown to have personalities that fit along these four continua. Indications of the child's personality help the team design the MSE. For example if the child is more extrovert than introvert, greater emphasis will need to be put on engagement with people rather than equipment. If the child is more intuitive than sensing, greater emphasis will need to be put on building trust and mutual respect rather than focusing purely on opening the child's sense window. If the child is more feeling than thinking, then greater emphasis will need to be put on enjoyment. If the child is more perceiving than judging, then greater emphasis will need to be put on learning by doing.

Interests are the things a person enjoys, the person's likes or preferences. Examining the things a person enjoys tells us about that person's personality. Such information is useful when designing the MSE. There are four main ways to collect information about a child's interests (Super 1957). They are:

- *Expressed interests* are statements of interest made by the child. Compose a list of activities where the child indicates enjoyment.
- *Manifest interests* are those shown through actions and participation. Compose a list of activities the child actually chooses to do.
- *Inventoried interests* are estimates of interest based on responses to questions concerning the child's likes and dislikes. Compose a list during the parents/caregivers questionnaire. Obtain additional information from significant others listing what they think the child likes or dislikes.
- *Tested interests* are those revealed under controlled situations. The MSE provides an ideal controlled environment in which to test the child's interests. The goal here is to extend the depth, breadth and balance of the child's interests.

Temperament refers to the how of behaviour rather than the what or why. Temperament is a behavioural style. Differences in temperament are present at birth. These differences influence how the individual behaves within an environment and how that individual is affected by that environment. Risk factors for emotional and behavioural problems emerge when there is a mismatch in the environmental demands made on the child and the child's temperament, the so it is important to have a clear understanding of the child's temperament. Temperament is a significant factor in childhood growth, health and development.

There are nine characteristics of temperament (Carey and McDevitt 1978). They are:

- **Activity level** – amount of physical activity during the day.
- **Regularity** – extent which patterns are consistent, eating, sleeping.
- **Approach-withdrawal** – response to novel situations.
- **Adaptability** – ease to change behaviour in a socially desirable direction.
- **Intensity** – amount of energy exhibited in emotional expressions.
- **Mood** – quality of emotional expression.
- **Persistence** – extent of uninterrupted continuation of behaviour.
- **Distractibility** – ease of interruption.
- **Sensory threshold** – sensitivity, degree individual reacts to environmental factors.

When assessing temperament in children with PMLD it is difficult to determine the boundary between temperament and learning difficulty. Therefore parents'/caregivers' input is particularly valuable.

Functional sense assessment

Three types of sense information are necessary for engagement with the external world. This information comes from:

- senses that inform the individual about their own internal world, namely the senses of proprioception – vestibular, muscle spindles and Golgi tendon organs;
- senses that inform the individual about their immediate world, namely the senses of near exteroception – olfactory, gustatory, the tactual and cutaneous senses;
- senses that inform the individual about the near to distant world, namely the senses of near to distant exteroception – hearing and vision.

Functional sense assessment involves identifying how well an individual uses each of the above senses for purposeful behaviour. This assessment begins with proprioception.

Proprioception

Proprioception or kinesthesia refers to the sensations of position, tension and movement of body parts. It is the intrinsic feedback mechanism that one uses to monitor one's own ability to maintain stability. The principal senses of proprioception include the vestibular system, muscle spindles and the Golgi tendon organs. Proprioception is closely connected with motor development. Motor development has therefore, also been included in this section.

The **vestibular system** is located in the inner ear. Sense organs in the vestibular system determine our ability to perceive rotary acceleration and orientation. There are three parts to the vestibular system. The first part is the semicircular canals. Angular acceleration causes fluid in the semicircular canals to bend hair cells which send neural messages to the brain. Parts two and three are concerned with orientation. Stone-like calcium deposits in the utricles and saccules respond to the pull of gravity and bend hair cells which send neural messages to the brain. The vestibular system enables the individual to keep the head in position and maintain an upright posture. It also helps the individual maintain a particular orientation with respect to his or her surroundings, which is valuable when learning how to engage with the external world.

There are also sense receptors in the joints, tendons and muscles. These provide the individual with sensations of position, tension and movement of body parts. Joint receptors respond to joint angles and to muscle force. Tendon receptors, which are located between the muscle and the bone, called the **Golgi tendon organs** respond to three types of changes in muscle force, a passive change when the muscle is pulled (as in massage), and two active changes: isometric and isotonic contractions. Muscle receptors in the form of **muscle spindles** maintain a two way communication with the central nervous system. Muscle spindles provide and receive information regarding changes in muscle length and muscle force.

The child achieves purposeful movement through integrated action of the sensory and motor areas of the central nervous system. These operate together on the skeletal structure. If the child has a physical disability, the struggle for the control of balance and movement can seriously deplete energy reserves. This then reduces the child's ability to concentrate on other matters.

The following assumptions about the maturation of the nervous system have been used when developing the MSE report on functional proprioception. They are:

- Children develop control over their bodies in progressions:
    cephalo-caudal (head-to-tail);
    proximo-distal (midline of trunk to fingers tips and toes);
    flexion to extension (bending at joints to straightening);
    undifferentiated responses to differentiated responses;
    reflexes to purposeful movement.
- Stimulation to the vestibular system helps to accelerate the rate of motor development.
- Vestibular stimulation comes from regular handling, being carried or through the use of movement-eliciting equipment.
- The experiences of the individual influence the way the brain develops. Proprioception experiences are important to brain development. Other influences include nutrition and genetics.
- Motor patterns simplify control. Motor patterns are a series of brain and spinal cord connections which are established through ongoing repetitions of the same or similar motor action. This repetition forms a functional feedback loop of connecting fibres in the nervous system to the brain.
- Sensory feedback helps the individual refine motor patterns.
- Memory about the environment, including the internal environment of the body, enables the individual's central and peripheral nervous system to draw anticipatory cues from motor experiences. This allows the individual to effectively predict movement outcomes. The process by which input from sensory receptors throughout the body is coordinated is called **sensory integration**. Coordination entails the association of sensory input with stored memories of prior experiences in order to produce adaptive responses.
- The goal of the educator is to help children with neuromotor impairments replace memories of unsuccessful movement experiences (ones where movement outcomes are not able to be effectively predicted) with self-initiated motor patterns that are more efficient and effective. Memories of huge numbers of unsuccessful movement experiences seem to clog the memory and make it difficult for the child to plan movements.
- Organised, sequenced and well-timed body adjustments and movements result in balance. Balance comes from *strength*, *mobility* and *stability*. Strength comes from the repetition of actions that require effort. Mobility is primarily achieved through appropriate positioning and physical support to facilitate independent movement. Stability needs to be both static and dynamic.

- Engagement with the external world through the senses provides a motivator for the child to develop balance.
- Sensorimotor development follows four sets of progressions:

    (1) extension against gravity – lifting head and straightening trunk while in prone position then lifting head and bending trunk while in supine position;

    (2) increasingly complex combinations of limb movements, random to coordinated bilateral arm and leg movements, to unilateral arm and leg movements, to diagonal arm and leg movements;

    (3) body movements through space, front-back, then side-to-side, then rotary;

    (4) large support base for balancing which progressively diminishes in size as equilibrium is achieved (Bly 1983).

- Children learn to move by actively engaging in the movement themselves, more than in passive exercises.
- Bone structure grows and develops in response to the way the child uses the body.
- Each movement requires a point of stability. The MSE team helps the child to move by highlighting the child's point of stability for that particular movement.
- Stable posture is built on symmetry. The aim is to improve symmetry and midline orientation during body movements.
- The goal is for movements against gravity to be fluid, efficient, automatic and variable.

When making the report on functional proprioception in the MSE (see Appendix 3), the child's current status is identified and a plan made to develop further muscle strength, mobility and stability in the light of current attainment. The point of stability for a new exercise should be identified. Attention should be paid to making the movement(s) as symmetrical as possible and active rather than passive. It the new proprioceptive experience is rejected by the child, try again another time. If persistent, develop another activity that is more closely related to the child's comfort zone.

Vignette – Skye

Skye does very few independent movements. We even have to strap her into her wheelchair to hold her upright. When we go into the MSE we move Skye out of her wheelchair and lie her on a large beach towel on the water bed. We then use the beach towel to roll Skye every ten minutes from supine to prone position. I use body signs to inform her when we are going to move her. I give her time to establish an equilibrium in the new position and then encourage her to engage in her prone position activity. Being in prone position, with her head at the end of the bed provides her with a good opportunity to use her vision. We place a soft toy dog on a mirror in front of Skye's eyes (15"/30cm) and she looks at the dog and herself in the mirror.

After ten minutes we roll Skye from prone to supine position. When she is lying on her back she can do a whole arm movement with her right arm and activate a wind chime. She does this activity for another ten minutes before we roll her back

---

on her tummy. I think the change is useful. She obviously enjoys both activities but the wind chime activity is tiring so the mirror activity gives her a little rest from physical activity. The turning is good for proprioception, there is the visual activity with the mirror and then we have the arm-eye coordination to activate the wind chime. I also think this activity is helping Skye develop or at least maintain some strength, stability and mobility.

Exteroception (near)

Exteroceptors are sense receptors that receive stimuli that enable us to detect, identify and locate objects in the external environment. There are two types of exteroceptors. Those that inform us about objects that are nearby and those that inform us about objects that are either nearby or distant. I will discuss taste, smell, touch and the cutaneous senses under the heading exteroception (near) and hearing and vision under the heading exteroception (near to distant). Clearly some senses more neatly fit into this classification than others. For example the cutaneous senses provide information about both the internal as well as the external worlds and smell allows us to identify objects in the distance as well as nearby.

Taste and smell

Taste and smell are often confused. This is because they both belong to the chemical sensing system called chemosensation. In addition to taste and smell we also have a third chemical sense which is located in the moist surfaces of the eyes, nose, mouth and throat. This sense identifies sensations such as the 'stinging' feeling associated with ammonia, the 'coolness' associated with menthol and the 'hot sensation' associated with chilli.

Taste (gustation) is a close sense. It is sometimes called the gatekeeper to the body because it provides us with information about substances in solutions that we eat or drink. Smell (olfaction) is a distant sense. It provides us with information about substances in gaseous form. Tastes, combined with a range of other sensations including temperature and texture, but particularly smell, form a common chemical sense called flavour. We use flavour to identify and recognise what we are eating. The fact that identifying flavour involves both taste and smell helps to explain why the two senses, taste and smell are often confused.

The chemosensation senses enable us to enjoy the delights of life, such as the smell of flowers or the flavours of foods and drinks. These senses also play an important role in helping to keep us safe. They warn us of impending danger, such as fire or pollution. They also let us know if our foods or drinks are poisonous.

Despite chemosensation disorders being relatively common (Bromley 2000), they are mostly ignored, particularly when they occur in children with PMLD. Chemosensation dysfunction is often associated with smell disturbance and it can and does negatively affect quality of life. As well as depriving the individual of sensual pleasures, there are associated adverse affects which relate to food choice and intake, weight loss, malnutrition, impaired immunity, depression and deterioration of general health. The three most common causes of chemosensation disorders are nasal and sinus disease, respiratory infection and brain damage. Other causes include medications, hormonal imbalance, dental problems, radiation, chemical pollution or poor nutrition.

Most taste buds are found on the tongue although they are also located in other parts of the mouth. The four main types of taste receptors are sweet (sugars) concentrated on the front tip of the tongue, salt front left and right sides, sour (acid) back left and right sides and bitter (alkaloids) central back.

Chemosensation is a strong motivator in the development of eating and drinking skills, such as sucking, chewing and swallowing. These activities encourage good muscle tone, a prerequisite for speech. Children with low muscle tone often have extremely limited chemosensation experiences, mainly because of health risks such as the possibility of choking and inability to swallow. Such children are dependent upon parents and/or carers to actively provide ongoing interesting taste and smell experiences.

Babies from a very early age can identify their mother through smell (especially if she is breast feeding). Young children can identify each family member by their distinctive odours. Smells signal the familiar: people, places and objects. They therefore play an important role in the development of memory.

For children with PMLD, chemosensation may be particularly critical in helping the child form a body scheme and to map the environment with respect to making observations about both location and time (see Appendix 2). What often happens in children with PMLD is that they tend to have very limited experience with smell and taste. They often form strong attachments with just a few flavours and reject everything else. This can make it extremely difficult to ensure that the child is receiving a nutritious and interesting diet.

Our job is to widen the child's taste and smell experiential base. We do this by providing the child with opportunities to experience a rich variety of taste and smell experiences. To do this we must establish a mutual relationship of trust and respect with the child. The key to establishing this relationship is to acknowledge that the child has a right to control what he or she eats and drinks. The best way we can help the child expand his or her taste and smell experiences is through gentle encouragement and fun.

If children are comfortable and enjoying themselves and are with people they know and trust then they are more likely to be open to new experiences – particularly if those new experiences are associated with a favourite, familiar experience. I think it is important to include taste and smell experiences in the MSE repertoire of activities. Besides, children need sustenance. Some children benefit from small but regular intake of food and drink. Food and drink provide the children with the energy they need to more actively engage in the learning activities that are provided in the MSE.

When assessing chemosensation (see Appendix 4) observe responses of the child to foods and drinks. Begin with a very small amount of food or drink on a familiar spoon or cup. This information will provide ideas to help encourage the child to expand his or her taste window. For example begin the meal with favourite food and then add a new taste sensation once the child is enjoying the eating experience. Use language to help the child anticipate and enjoy the experience. For example, 'We're going to taste something really yummy. I'll give you just a little bit to see what you think. Mmmm wasn't that nice. There I knew you'd like it. Do you want to have a little bit more?' Be conscious that language can interfere with the child developing skills during the acquisition and fluency stage. Avoid language during the actual tasting experience and wait for the child's response before commenting.

Are there any factors which might indicate a chemosensation disorder?

- Does the child have a respiratory infection? If so leave the assessment until the child is better.
- Does the child have any allergies? If so which ones? Important to know these so that they can be avoided when doing work with taste and smell.
- Does the child have a blocked nose? If so help the child to clear his or her nose. Wipe nose.
- Does the child have any dental problems? These need to be attended to as soon as possible.
- Does the child have any brain damage resulting in chemosensation dysfunction? If so, the child may only respond to enhanced flavours.

Observe responses of the child to smell. Start with a natural, familiar smell that is known to be liked from the parents/caregivers interview – for example, soap or a crushed herb such as mint. Use this experience to build trust and confidence. Then offer a new smell, either another natural smell or a cotton wool ball impregnated with an essential oil attached to a large peg that could be held by the child if the child has grasping skills. The smell will be accepted, ignored or rejected. If rejected, decide whether to try another smell or to close the session and reinvestigate smell another day. Rejected smells can be reoffered at a later stage. If the child makes a neutral response, reoffer the smell. It is best not to use language when the child is smelling as it seems to interfere with the smelling experience. Language is used though to cue the activities and to give the child feedback after the child has engaged in the smelling activity.

It is a good idea to build up a bank of information about the child's likes and dislikes regarding smell and taste. This information will be valuable during the programme development stage (see Chapter 3). It is also useful to observe what the child's taste and smell skill level is.

I have adapted Aitken and Buultjens' (1992) functional visual assessment to develop similar stages in taste and smell. These stages help give the educator some ideas regarding how to structure a functional chemosensation programme. The stages reflect increasingly sophisticated chemosensation abilities. They are:

- *Chemosensation awareness* – Is the child aware of tastes and smells?
- *Chemosensation attending* – Is the child attending to different tastes and smells?

- *Chemosensation localising* – Is the child localising tastes and smells (does he or she realise that certain smells are associated with certain objects, certain tastes are associated with certain foods)?
- *Chemosensation recognising* – Is the child able to recognise certain tastes and smells (if so which ones)?
- *Chemosensation understanding* – Is the child able to understand the significance of a taste or a smell (an orange has a particular taste and smell and it is always the same)?

Vignette – Francine

Francine likes the smell of patchouli oil. Her mother sometimes wears it so it's a familiar smell for Francine and it makes her feel secure. When we first introduced Francine to the MSE we established a certain bean bag as a comfort zone for her – and we put a little pillow with patchouli on it in a pocket sewn into the bean bag. We follow a set routine. The first thing we do when we go into the MSE is help Francine to her bean bag. It's her place. It has her favourite smell. Then Francine begins to explore the MSE from her comfort zone. I think smell is a powerful part of the process for Francine. Her mother says Francine is very close to her Nana and she wears lavender. Next time I establish a comfort zone in the MSE I'm going to add a lavender scent pocket. It will be interesting to see if Francine can differentiate between the two locations using smell.

Tactual and cutaneous senses

The tactual and cutaneous senses include the receptors of touch, pressure temperature (thermoreceptors) and pain (nociceptors). The term 'tactile' is used to refer to passive touch such as the sensation of a bean bag under the child's back. The term 'haptic' is used to indicate that the experience is active rather than passive touch.

Haptic (active) touch involves both contact information via the skin and proprioceptive information via movement and joint position. When we hold an apple, the position of our fingers around the apple tells us as much about it as our skin does. Learning through the tactual sense therefore actually involves learning through a combination of somatosensory senses namely: proprioception, touch and the cutaneous senses. Haptic touch using the finger tips also requires significant levels of motor development.

Functional touch is any use of touch that adds to the child's experience, enjoyment and learning about the world. Touch is enormously important in human activity. It is an essential component in learning how to manipulate and shape of the world. Touch involves the discrimination of:

- textures (rough to smooth);
- density (hard to soft);
- state (gas to fluid to solid);
- surface to depth (palpation);

- size (small to large);
- temperature (hot to cold);
- vibration (static to gentle to vigorous);
- shape (circle, square).

Tactual exploration is a sequential process where one part is joined to other parts to provide an overall impression of the whole. This means that a large number of sophisticated skills are involved, including the higher order functions of memory, spatial ability, gross and fine motor development and scanning.

If you are working with a child who resists using their hands, the best solution is to move back to functional proprioception activities. These activities help establish trust and make touch and movement fun. Reciprocal whole-body interactions such as rocking, swinging and bouncing also provide the foundation for communication because the adult follows the child's lead by bouncing or swinging or rocking for a short period of time and then only recontinuing when the child indicates that more is required.

Smith and Levack (1996) proposed a seven stage sequence of tactual development which provides a valuable template on which to collect information about the child's tactual development when designing the MSE (see Appendix 5). The stages are:

- *Tactual locating* – involves a random or intentional search for something. For example a baby uses the mouth to locate the mother's nipple during breast feeding.
- *Tactual exploring* – involves making hand movements over something to find out about its tactual qualities. Often during breast feeding the baby will move the hand over the mother's skin to explore the feel of the mother's skin.
- *Tactual manipulating* – involves the intentional movement of an object. The baby may grasp the mother's hair and then pull it.
- *Tactual recognising* – involves associating an object with a memory. Babies who are bottle fed recognise the bottle and its teat by touch.
- *Tactual comparing* – involves identifying similarities and differences in the way different things feel. Once children can make tactual comparisons they are able to show preferences, match items and categorise them. They also may reject items that are different.
- *Tactual communicating* – involves using tactual objects to inform other people. For example the child may use a cup to request a drink.
- *Tactual organising* – involves using touch to find objects, to allocate a set place for them and to recognise a set task for them.

When children with PMLD are not helped to use and enjoy their sense of touch they may become tactile defensive or tactile avoidant. This means they avoid the sensation of unfamiliar textures, particularly ones that are sticky or gooey. Many children with PMLD have very limited experiences with objects. Often they form strong attachment to a particular object and reject all other objects so it becomes a vicious circle. Involvement with this single object, though intense tends to be nonfunctional and highly repetitive so in effect the stereotyped behaviour becomes a barrier to the child learning functional touch.

The goal is to help the child with PMLD learn through touch. This involves making the child's tactual window as wide as possible by providing a variety of rich tactual experiences. These experiences help the child learn to use the hands confidently and competently to access meaningful information about the world.

Such a process involves the careful and deliberate establishment of a supportive tactual learning environment. This is built on the development of a trusting relationship with the child, where the child knows that he or she has the right to control what is touched. The MSE team must demonstrate that the child is in charge, that the child controls what is touched, the length of time touching occurs, and when touching will cease. A supportive tactual learning environment also contains things that the child likes to touch.

The development of touch in children with PMLD is best facilitated by being encouraging but never demanding. The child's behaviour is indicative of where the child is at developmentally. Forcing the child does more harm than good. Learning begins when the educator offers the child an object to touch by making a sound with it or by putting it in contact with the child's arm or leg. The child will let you know it he or she wishes to touch the object by grasping for it. If the child rejects your offer, try another object. Rejected objects can be reoffered at some later stage. If the child makes a neutral response, repeat the offer.

Tactual development can also be encouraged using parallel play. This involves the adult following the child's lead using a second object. The play gradually evolves into turn taking and then to interaction using a shared object. Another method to promote tactual development involves the use of modelling where the adult places a hand under the child's hand then tactually explores the object.

Be careful with the way language is used when teaching the child to learn through touch particularly during the acquisition and fluency stages. Language can interfere with the child's focus. Always seek the child's permission before taking the child's hand. This can be done tactually by putting your hand on top of the child's hand and only proceeding if the child does not remove his or her hand. It is also important to inform the child with PMLD what you plan to do next. For example 'time to eat' can be cued by showing the child a spoon.

Exteroception (near to distant)

Hearing

Functional hearing is the use of any hearing a child might have which could add to the child's experience, enjoyment and learning about the world. Even small amounts of hearing can provide the child with valuable information about the world, as long as the child is able to interpret it in a meaningful way. For example the child might have enough hearing to be able to hear the beat of a bass drum. Whatever hearing the child has is potentially valuable.

In this section I will use the term educationally deaf to refer to a child who does not have measurable functional hearing. The term hard of hearing will be used to refer to a child who, even after correction, still experiences significant difficulty with hearing. The term limited hearing refers to a child who, after hearing correction, has normal functional hearing.

Even though the child may have the potential to hear, the child may not have learnt how to use this hearing in meaningful ways and may need to be explicitly taught to develop functional hearing skills. In children with PMLD auditory functioning can often be improved by closely matching the quality and quantity of auditory experiences with the needs of the child. It is important to be begin these activities when the child is very young. The earlier these auditory experiences are provided, the better the chances are that the child's auditory functioning will improve.

Matching the quality and quantity of auditory experiences with the needs of the child involves finding out about the child's hearing (see Appendix 6). Begin by obtaining an up to date medical report. This would be provided by an otorhinolaryngologist, a surgeon who specialises in diagnosing and treating ear conditions. You will also require an up to date audiologist's report on the child's hearing in the form of an audiogram. Hearing loss is recorded on an audiogram, a grid system where the x-axis indicates frequency which is measured in hertz (Hz) and the y-axis indicates volume which is measured in decibels (dB).

It is important to be aware of the child's hearing loss and compare how this relates to the amount of hearing required for regular speech.

- *Mild hearing loss* is between 20 to 40 decibels. Such a loss makes it difficult for individuals to recognise that someone is addressing them.
- *Moderate hearing loss* is between 40 to 65 decibels. Such a loss makes it difficult for the person to understand speech unless the person is able to closely watch the speaker's face.
- *Severe hearing loss* is between 65 to 95 decibels. Such a loss makes normal conversation virtually impossible.
- *Profound hearing loss* is a loss of 95 decibels or greater. Such a loss means that the individual is very dependent upon other senses for information about the world.

The audiologist is a non-medical practitioner who prescribes hearing aids. The audiologist will provide audiograms (see Figure 2.1) which show the child's hearing before and after correction. Nowadays even young babies and children with PMLD can have their hearing tested, using either a brainstem auditory-evoked response test which measures brain waves or an acoustic immittance test which measures the response of hair cells in the inner ear to external sounds. This means that much more precisely calibrated hearing aids can be prescribed for children with PMLD.

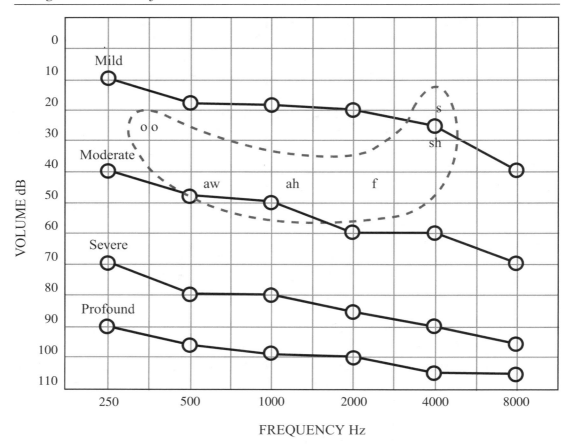

Figure 2.1 The speech sound 'banana' superimposed on an audiogram showing mild, moderate, severe and profound hearing loss. Adpated from Power (1998) pp. 348, 356.

It is also important to obtain up to date information about the child's hearing from the school file because people who live and work with the child often make valuable observations about the child's functional hearing.

Hearing loss due to the ear rather than the brain is called **auricular hearing loss**. **Conductive hearing loss** relates to a hearing problem in the middle or external ear which results in low frequency hearing loss and a volume loss up to 60 dB (mild to moderate range). **Sensorineural hearing loss** relates to a hearing problem in the inner ear and can result in severe to profound deafness. A combination of conductive and sensorineural hearing loss is called a **mixed hearing loss**.

Central hearing loss is hearing loss due to the brain rather than the ear. **Cortical hearing loss** implies the damage is related to the auditory cortex. In addition to damage to the auditory cortex, there may be cognitive problems, where auditory information cannot be processed meaningfully. Sounds are heard but not understood. This may be more common in children with PMLD than previously thought.

As with functional chemosensation, I have adapted Aitken and Buultjens' (1992) functional visual assessment to develop corresponding stages of functional hearing assessment. These stages provide the educator with ideas regarding how to structure a functional hearing programme when working with children, who due to the PMLD, particularly those with central hearing loss, show few concrete signs of ever being able to acquire speech. The stages of functional hearing are:

- *Auditory awareness* – the child shows some sign that he or she is obtaining some auditory information. These signs needs to be recorded and used to describe what the child can and cannot hear.
- *Auditory attending* – the child is able to make sufficient auditory differentiation to be able to concentrate on listening to something.
- *Auditory localising* – the child is able to consistently differentiate a particular auditory event and maybe even identify where a sound is coming from.
- *Auditory recognising* – the child is able to isolate a particular feature of a sound and is able to match it with a past memory of that sound. For example can the child make two drum beats after you beat the drum twice?
- *Auditory understanding* – the child understands the relevance, significance and use of hearing. For example wants you to make three drum beats after he/she makes three drum beats.

Vision

Functional vision is the use of any vision the child might have, no matter how slight, which can add to the child's 'experience, enjoyment and learning about the world' (Aitken and Buultjens 1992).

If the child only has light perception this means the child will have sufficient vision to be able to tell the difference between night and day or when a room is or is not lit. Any vision is potentially useful.

Even though a child might have the potential to be able to see the child may not have learnt how to use this potential in meaningful ways. The child may need to be explicitly taught to see.

In children with PMLD, with the right exercises, visual functioning can often be improved. Visual functioning is improved by closely matching the quality and quantity of visual experiences with the needs of the child. It is important to begin these activities when the child is very young. The earlier these visual experiences are provided the better the chances are that the child's visual functioning will improve.

Begin your functional vision report (see Appendix 7) by obtaining:

- an up to date ophthalmological report on the child's vision;
- an up to date optometrical report on the child's vision;
- current corrective vision aids (e.g., spectacles);
- up to date information about the child from the school file.

If the above information is not available then request that the child be tested and that appropriate vision aids be prescribed. The formal visual assessment reports will let you know where, on the point of the visual continuum to start your assessment of functional vision.

The child may have:

- **Ocular visual impairment** which means there is some damage to the eyes.
- **Cortical visual impairment** (CVI) which means there is some damage to the brain.
- Problems interpreting visual information at the cognitive level. This may relate to lack of visual experience.
- Combinations of the above (common in children with PMLD).

If the child has an ocular visual impairment the child's vision may range from:

- **Educationally blind** which means no functional vision is available for learning.
- **Partially sighted/low vision** which means after correction some functional vision is available for learning.
- **Visually limited** which means after correction normal functional vision is available for learning.

Important visual skills for education (Alchin and Pagliano 1988) include:

- *Field of vision*, which is the area that a person can see when looking straight ahead.
- *Distance visual acuity*, which is the ability to clearly and sharply discern an object in the distance.
- *Near visual acuity*, which is the ability to clearly and sharply discern an object close up.
- *Stereopsis or depth perception*, which requires binocular vision, the coordinated functioning of both eyes.
- *Colour vision*, which is the ability to detect different hues particularly in the red-green range.
- *Accommodative and fusional vergence*, which is the ability of the eyes to maintain focus at near range and to change focus quickly and accurately.
- *Ocular motility*, which includes *saccades*, quick accurate movements used to jump from one object to another and *tracking*, smooth accurate eye movements.
- *Near point of convergence* is the ability to point both eyes exactly at the same nearby object at the same time.

If the child has CVI, the type of vision loss is going to be influenced by the type of brain damage and the brain's ability to compensate for this damage. Visual functioning in children with CVI can be enormously variable both within the same child, perhaps even within short time intervals, and between different children. Additional factors which may influence the child's vision include motivation, emotion, stress, fatigue and medications. It is important to think of each child in terms of an individual rather than in terms of the disability. Educators need to make close observations of each child and keep records of the child's progress.

Many children with PMLD have a range of visual problems that may or may not include both ocular and cortical visual impairment. They may have spent extended periods not using or under utilising their vision so they may also lack visual experience and they may experience difficulties interpreting visual information at the cognitive level.

While children with CVI are often attracted to bright lights and bright colours, up to one third of children with CVI are photophobic. Educators therefore need to closely observe which lighting conditions best suit the child. Rapid head shaking or eye poking is not common in children with CVI. These behaviours are more often related to ocular visual impairment.

Colour vision is often preserved in children with CVI because colour perception involves bilateral brain functions. The child is therefore likely to show a preference for colour, especially yellow and red and find visual activities that are black and white much more difficult to see. Depth perception is often poor because it requires cerebral coordination of binocular vision. Children with CVI may become overwhelmed by a visual experience. Educators therefore need to factor in regular opportunities for the child to recover his or her composure during visual stimulation activities. This could be achieved by:

• brief exposure to the stimulus followed by a rest period;
• opportunities for the child to look away then look back;
• support for the child to monitor and control the amount of visual stimulation he or she is comfortable with.

Learning how to see can be hard work for the child with CVI so it is important to give the child regular opportunities to rest. At the same time it is necessary to allow the child sufficient time to see and respond to the visual stimulation. The educator therefore needs to make very close observation of the child's visual needs, and be informed by the child's microresponses such as breathing patterns, shifts in gaze and body position. Learning how to see can be so demanding of the child's energy that it may be necessary to separate tasks such as using vision, head control and fine motor activities. The energy used to control one's head may inhibit the child's ability to concentrate on the visual stimulation. It is similar to you walking up ten flights of stairs while patting your head with one hand and rubbing your tummy in a circular motion with the other, using goggles which provide never before seen abstract visual messages. The more physically tired you become, the more difficult it is to coordinate the task. A head support may help the child. The child may also find it helpful to have a drink or to eat something in between tasks to replenish energy supplies. As with all other functional sense activities only check momentum after acquisition, fluency and endurance have been achieved.

Familiarity, simplicity, consistency, and repetition are the best strategies. Reduce visual clutter in the environment. For that matter reduce all non-relevant environmental stimulation. Be as consistent as possible, especially when stimulating vision. Keep colour, time and locations consistent, for example if the child can see yellow use exactly the same yellow bowl for all meals at home, at school and in the community. Repetitions and routines therefore become an important part of the visual programme. This helps the child build up a visual memory.

Short regular exercises that are fun for the child are best. This is achieved by taking into account the child's personality – what does the child like – e.g., what is his or her favourite size or colour? If the child wants to get very close to see an object that is acceptable. Use movement to help the child to see more easily, particularly when the child is using his or her visual field. Some children who look using their visual field appear as if they are looking away, when they are actually trying to line up the image on the retina so let children adopt whatever posture best suits them.

Positioning of the child is important. Try to observe which position is best for the child. Prone position is often a good viewing position. Be careful not to make other demands on the child's energy. A head support may be useful but remember the head support may make it more difficult for the child to look away when the stimulation is overwhelming.

Use consistent language to help the child develop and use functional vision. Children are often able to see better when they are told in advance what to look for.

Use multisensory approaches, pairing touch, sounds or movement with vision to support visual development. Be careful to identify when a particular multisensory stimulus is appropriate and constructive and when it is distracting.

Aitken and Buultjens (1992) proposed the use of five increasingly more complex stages as the basis of conducting a functional vision assessment. These stages also give the educator some ideas regarding how to structure the functional vision programme. They are:

- *Visual awareness* – the child shows some sign that he or she is obtaining some visual information.
- *Visual attending* – the child is able to make sufficient visual differentiation to be able to visually concentrate on something.
- *Visual localising* – the child is able to consistently differentiate a particular visual event.
- *Visual recognising* – the child is able to isolate a particular feature of an object and is able to match it with a past memory of that object.
- *Visual understanding* – the child visually understands the relevance, significance and use of an object.

Engagement and communication

Bunning (1998) classified behaviour in terms of engagement and purpose. The goal when using the MSE is to reduce the amount of non-purposeful adaptive behaviour and to increase the amount of purposeful adaptive behaviour. For a copy of the Engagement Report see Appendix 8.

Individuals purposefully engage with objects, people and events through their sense windows. An example of object-engagement (purposeful interaction with an object) is playing with a fibre-optic spray. A sophisticated subset of object-engagement is being aware of object permanence, an awareness that an object exists even when it is out of perceptual contact. An example of person-engagement (purposeful interaction with another person) is interaction with a teacher or a peer. The child might make eye contact with the adult and smile. Object-person-engagement is when the purposeful interaction is with both a person and an object, for example, when two children are placed in the ball pool and they pass a ball from one to the other. Event-engagement refers to the individual participating in a particular event such as having a massage. Engagement was subdivided into five levels of involvement: orientation, responsiveness, reciprocation, initiative and association (Bunning 1996). The following questions help the educator identify which level the child has reached.

- **Orientation**: Has information about an offer to engage been received? Does the child stop self-stimulation in response to the offer to engage?
- **Responsiveness**: Does the child respond to received sense information? Is the response positive, neutral or negative?
- **Reciprocation**: Is there an interchange of interaction, i.e. turn taking?
- **Initiative**: Is the child adding new information?
- **Association**: Is the child making a connection of some kind, e.g. generalising, aware of object permanence, linking people and events?

According to Bunning (1998) non-purposeful adaptive behaviour may be in the form of:

- **Non-engagement.** This refers to a body action where the individual is not conscious. These actions might occur during sleep, deep rest, as a result of sedation or during an epileptic fit.
- **Self-neutral engagement.** This refers to routine body movements that happen spontaneously during waking hours such as sitting, yawning, walking or scratching one's head.
- **Self-active engagement.** This refers to any behaviour that lacks a clear purpose, is characterised by compulsive or repetitive actions that provide predictable feedback to the individual but are not relevant to what is happening outside that individual. They are more commonly referred to as stereotyped behaviours.

Stereotyped behaviours

The term stereotyped behaviours is used to describe certain behaviours that are associated with different types and combinations of disabilities, particularly autism, sensory disabilities, severe learning difficulties and PMLD.

Stereotyped behaviour is any persistent, highly repetitive or compulsive action which is irrelevant to activities outside the individual, is apparently meaningless but provides predictable feedback to the individual. Excessive rocking is an example of a stereotyped behaviour. Stereotyped behaviours have a wide variety of forms and can be described in terms of their intensity, frequency, duration and consequence. Different terms are used to describe particular characteristics of the stereotyped behaviour. These include: blindism, challenging behaviour, maladaptive behaviour, mannerisms, obsessive behaviour, problem behaviour, ritualistic behaviour, self-active engagement, self-injurious behaviour and self-stimulation. There has been a

57

long history of these terms being imprecisely defined and so their meanings have tended to be user-dependent. To cut through this, I divide stereotyped behaviours into three broad categories: self-stimulation, problem behaviours and challenging behaviours.

Self-stimulation refers to persistent, highly repetitive mannerisms unlikely to have adverse sequelae. For example, John may gently tap his finger on his wrist while he is waiting for the bus each morning, while Julie doodles. The only difference is John has a vision impairment and has worked out a different way of fidgeting. Rocking could also be described as self-stimulation. When certain stereotyped behaviours such as rocking are closely associated with vision impairment they are called blindisms. Self-stimulation is not necessarily undesirable as it can help maintain alertness.

Problem behaviours are stereotyped behaviours that interfere with learning and development. The mannerism becomes so all consuming that the individual is cut off from the external world. Rocking is only a problem behaviour when the individual is obsessive, going to extreme lengths to do the behaviour and finds it almost impossible to stop. Problem behaviour needs addressing by the MSE team.

Challenging behaviours include self-injurious behaviour and those that exclude the child from the community. Self-injurious behaviour is defined as 'any self-inflicted action that results in bruising, lacerations, lesions, callouses, skin breakdown, or other injury on the individual's own body' (Turner *et al.* 1996, p. 312). According to Emerson *et al.* (1988) a severely challenging behaviour is a 'behaviour of such intensity, frequency or duration that the physical safety of the person or others is likely to be placed in serious jeopardy, or behaviour which is likely to seriously limit or deny access to and use of ordinary community facilities'. Rocking would only be thought of as challenging if some damage or injury was occurring or if it was used as a reason to exclude the child from participating in community activities. Challenging behaviours need to be urgently addressed by the MSE team. These categories of self-stimulation, problem and challenging behaviours are context dependent, i.e. the same behaviour but in another context may be categorised differently.

The assumption is that children with PMLD use stereotyped behaviours to compensate for lack of meaningful sensory stimulation. The MSE can help break the cycle by providing an opportunity to help the child use his or her remaining senses to participate in and to make sense of the world. Engagement with objects, people and events in the MSE helps the child form concepts about the world. The MSE provides a special environment that is built on the establishment of trust and mutual respect. It offers the child consistency and predictability which provides the child with opportunities to develop a sense of control over the environment. By engaging with objects, people and events in the MSE, the child makes bonds which support the child in taking risks. This provides the basis for developing a dialogue with the external world.

Assumptions about behaviour

The following assumptions have been made about the behaviour of children with PMLD.

- Identifying the child with PMLD's abilities and behaviours provides the most useful way to develop a programme for use in the MSE. The PMLD makes it difficult to identify the individual child's abilities and interests and makes it particularly difficult to predict how the individual child is likely to behave.
- Children with PMLD often respond to the natural environment in unusual ways. Some children limit their sense use, e.g. become tactile defensive, only eat certain things, and some become locked in repetitive, self-stimulatory behaviours.
- Children with PMLD are likely to focus on themselves. Their learning difficulties make it extremely difficult for them to purposefully engage with objects, people and events in the external world. They need explicit help to be able to engage in purposeful ways.
- Children with PMLD depend strongly on routines and repetition. These help the child feel comfortable, make accurate predictions about the world and facilitate learning. Educators should be careful to design learning experiences that use routines and repetition as a basis for learning.
- Combined impairments in memory, reasoning, hearing and vision mean the child has little understanding of space and the environment. This seriously inhibits the child's willingness to move and explore. Lack of sensory input further reduces the child's motivation to engage with a seemingly chaotic and unpredictable external world. Children learn to move and explore by engaging in highly repetitive and predictable movement activities such as rocking and swinging. To be a successful activity, movement from one location to another must involve more pleasant than unpleasant experiences, more familiar than unfamiliar experiences and change that is introduced in small increments. When the child learns to move from one location to another it is best to establish comfort zones for the child and to make bridges between the two zones built using familiar experiences.

Assumptions about communication

There are three components of communication. These are:

- **Form** – the vehicle for conveying meaning.
- **Social aspects** – the reason for communicating.
- **Content** – what the child communicates about.

PMLD means that the child is exposed to fewer forms. The vehicle for conveying meaning is going to be determined by the child's sense windows to the world. For example if the child is deaf and blind, communication will need to be tactual. The form is further limited by the cognitive development of the child.

PMLD makes it difficult for the child to develop bonds with the external world (i.e. engage with objects, people and events). This will slow down the development of communicative intent and limit the number of communicative functions the individual will be able to engage in.

PMLD also limits what the child will be able to communicate about. A big problem is that many experiences in the natural world are fragmented and limited. The MSE provides an opportunity for the child's world to be more controlled and predictable.

When preparing the MSE Functional Communication Report (see Appendix 9) prepare a personal communication portfolio which identifies the child's communication level.

Accidental communication is when the child makes a reflex reaction which indicates how the child feels. When the reflex action occurs, describe the behaviour and indicate what it might mean. For example the child might spit out food on taste. This reflex action could possibly mean: 'I don't like the taste' or 'I'm not hungry'. The educator then needs to consider an appropriate response to bridge communication to make it more intentional. For example, the educator could say or sign (or both) 'Yucky?' or 'Not hungry?'.

Pre-intentional communication is when the child shows some awareness of their own reaction. When such a behaviour occurs describe the behaviour and indicate what it might mean. For example a child may spit the food out and then refuse to reopen his or her mouth. This gives a message that the child is aware of his or her own reaction. The educator needs to make this communication less ambiguous, more precise. To do this the educator might say or sign (or both) 'No food. Like a drink?'.

Intentional communication is when the child is proactive. When the child makes a proactive communicative behaviour, the educator should describe the behaviour and indicate what it might mean. For example the child might smile and open his or her mouth when asked 'Would you like a drink?'. If this occurred the educator would need to consider an appropriate response to reinforce this behaviour. This could include congratulating the child for making his or her wish clear by saying or signing (or both) 'Yes you want a drink'. Then the drink should be provided immediately.

Summary

Children with PMLD require specialised assessment. The assessor must have exceptional skills of observation and interpretation, and these skills will only come from having an indepth knowledge of the area and of the child. Assessment provides a comprehensive audit of the child's current ability and circumstance. Nine types of assessment intermesh in the MSE: ecological, judgement based, process, interactive, adaptive-to-handicap, curriculum based, norm based and play assessments plus systematic observation.

Assessment for the MSE is divided into three core areas: the parents/caregivers interview and questionnaire, functional sense assessment, and assessment of engagement and communication. The parents/caregivers questionnaire gathers general and specific information about the child including personality, interests and temperament as well as the child's social context. The questionnaire is deliberately semi-structured with open questions. It is the entry point for parents/caregivers to be on the MSE team.

Functional sense assessment is made of the proprioceptive and the near and distant exteroceptive systems, to identify how well the individual uses these senses for purposeful behaviour. Distant exteroception is predicated on near exteroception and near exteroception is predicated on proprioception. Proprioception refers to the sensation of position, tension and movement of body parts. Stimulation of the vestibular system helps to accelerate the rate of motor development. Sensory feedback refines motor patterns. Proprioceptive development follows four sets of progression: extension against gravity, increasingly complex combinations of muscle group activity, body movements through space and balance. Balance comes from strength, mobility and stability.

Near exteroception involves chemosensation (smell and taste) and tactual and cutaneous senses. Chemosensation is a strong motivator in the development of eating and drinking skills, such as sucking, chewing and swallowing. These activities encourage muscle tone which is a prerequisite for speech. Tactual and cutaneous senses follow seven stages: locating, exploring, manipulating, recognising, comparing, communicating and organising. Tactual exploration is a sequential process involving sophisticated skills such as higher order memory, spatial ability, gross and fine motor development and scanning.

Distant exteroception involves hearing and vision and considerably enlarges the size of the child's perceived world. As for chemosensation, functional auditory and visual ability follows five sequential stages: awareness, attending, localising, recognising and understanding. Medical intervention and aids can substantially improve functional distant exteroception.

In assessing functional senses, use language prior to cue, so the child can anticipate the activity, but not during the sense experience as it can be distracting for the child. Start from familiar sense experiences before offering a new one. Allow the child to accept, ignore or reject the new sense experience. If ignored, offer it again. If rejected, consider whether to try another sense experience or to close the session and reinvestigate another time. Rejected sense experiences can be offered at a later stage. It is important to encourage the child to be self-determining and to respect his or her choices.

The final core area of assessment is that of engagement and communication. Purposeful engagement is with objects, people and events. Engagement can be divided into five levels of involvement: orientation, responsiveness, reciprocation, initiative and association. Non-purposeful adaptive behaviour may be non-engagement, self-neutral engagement and self-active engagement. Self-active engagement consists of stereotyped behaviours that develop to compensate for lack of meaningful sensory stimulation. Stereotyped behaviours can be categorised as self-stimulation, problem behaviour (interfering with learning and development) and challenging behaviour (resulting in injury to person and/or property and/or community exclusion). Combined impairments in memory, reasoning, hearing and vision can seriously inhibit the child's willingness to move and explore in a seemingly chaotic and unpredictable world. Communication is the highest order cognitive process addressed in the MSE and has three components: form, social aspects and content. Communication is categorised as being accidental, pre-intentional or intentional.

3 Instructional strategies and methods in the MSE

What are instructional strategies and methods?

An **instructional strategy** is an approach to teaching. Strategy is 'skilful management in… attaining an end' (*Macquarie Concise Dictionary* 1997). Instructional strategies are associated with the big picture view of teaching. The idea of the MSE being an 'open-minded' or a multifunctional space for leisure, therapy and education is part of the big picture view, as is the idea of having MSE design prototypes and using them to construct a hybrid MSE to suit the child's individualised sensory plan. On a smaller scale an instructional strategy is also used during a lesson to achieve a particular learning outcome. For example, having an educator work one-to-one with a child is an instructional strategy that is often used in the MSE. During this one-to-one correspondence the educator becomes a facilitator, providing opportunities for the individual to make inquiries about the world, to make choices, to engage in daily living tasks, to be productive, to enjoy human creativity, to make connections and to influence and shape the world. Another instructional strategy that is used in the MSE is to match task difficulty with the child's sense ability. The educator controls stimulation in ways that match the child's learning needs, to help the child with PMLD learn how to make meaning of the world using his or her senses. In particular the educator will use the nine stages for a child to learn new skills discussed in Chapter 1: preacquisition, acquisition, fluency, endurance, momentum, generalisation, adaptation, retention and maintenance.

An **instructional method** addresses the here and now of the small picture view of teaching. Method is 'a way of doing something, esp [sic] in accordance with a definite plan' (*Macquarie Concise Dictionary* 1997). Instructional methods describe the actions of the MSE team when teaching.

Good teaching for all children involves making matches between the child's ability and task difficulty. The difference between the ordinary classroom and the MSE, however, comes into focus when we think about the teaching-learning paradigm. For most children who arrive at school, their ability to engage with the environment is well established. The environment plays solely an extension role in the teaching-learning paradigm. When children with PMLD arrive at school, many are not able to engage in the multisensory aspects of the natural environment in purposeful or meaningful ways. This means that the environment plays an essential role in the teaching-learning paradigm. Instead of just making a match between the child's ability and the task, a third factor now enters the equation, namely the environment.

A **programme-environment-individual** fit is achieved by carefully identifying the child's sense windows and engineering the environment accordingly. In Chapter 1 we looked at a range of equipment and design prototypes that could be used to engineer the environment to achieve particular outcomes. In Chapter 2 we focused on ways to help us more accurately describe the child's sense windows. Now, in Chapter 3 we will examine the programme part of the fit.

Building the MSE from the child out

The MSE is built from the child out. The team constructs the MSE, and plans and implements activities in the MSE to take account of the child's:

- sense abilities;
- personality, temperament, interests, likes and dislikes;
- degree of engagement and communication skills;
- age and sociocultural background.

The goal of the MSE is to provide opportunities for the child to make sense of the world, by engaging with objects, people and events in meaningful ways. An important part of this process is being able to communicate.

The method of communication used by the child will depend on the child's sense abilities. Speech is dependent on the child having adequate hearing and the physical skills to reproduce sound. Sign language and the use of picture symbols are dependent on the child having vision and well developed fine motor skills. Even tactile finger spelling is dependent upon the child having a relatively well developed cognitive ability. This leaves a small group of children with PMLD, the ones who often use the MSE, with very few communication options available to them. Joint (2001) has developed a communication method which uses tactile signs on the child's body. These body signs are based on common sign language signs but have been modified so that they can be located on the child's body. Developing a communication system that is within the sensory and cognitive remit of the child is a challenge for the MSE team and that can only be addressed by the team being systematic in its approach.

Comfort zones

Brannock and Golding (2000) have developed a method to teach orientation and mobility to children with visual impairment. This method begins with the child establishing comfort zones. The teacher helps the child establish a comfort zone by directing the child to become aware of the place or space through a series of 'nearby considerations'. I have adapted the Brannock and Golding method for use in the MSE with children with PMLD. Each nearby consideration links a body part with a sense message.

- **Feet** – What can the child touch under the feet?
- **Hands** – What can the child touch through the hands?
- **Nose** – What can the child smell?
- **Ears** – What can the child hear?
- **Eyes** – What can the child see?

Other nearby considerations that could be used are:

- **Face** – What can the child feel on the face?
- **Front** – What can the child feel on the front?
- **Back** – What can the child feel on his or her back?

I advocate establishing a comfort zone by:

- Basing it on the observed interests, likes and preferences of the child as well as on the child's sense abilities.
- Constructing the comfort zone before the child comes into the room.
- Using a script for settling the child into the comfort zone.
- Accompanying each nearby consideration with an unchanging scripted auditory and tactual commentary to enrich the experience and to provide a basis for communication development. (See Chapter 4 for an example of a comfort zone being set up in practice.)

I advocate deliberately constructing two distinctive comfort zones within the MSE. These two comfort zones provide the child with two well established bases from which to explore the MSE.

Success versus frustration

Children learn best by achieving success. The more success a child achieves, the more willing that child is to take risks and try to learn new things. Success can therefore breed success. A realisation that success is possible can also motivate the child to want to persevere with a task, despite frustration.

Children with PMLD achieve very little success. For these children every learning activity is difficult, every learning activity is highly frustrating. The MSE provides an opportunity for the educator to significantly reduce frustration levels and to promote success through careful engineering of the environment.

I think the child with PMLD needs to bathe under a waterfall of success in the MSE for as long as it takes for that child to decide he or she wants to come out of his or her comfort zone to begin to explore the rest of the MSE. Tasks are generated that are known to be well within the range of the child's abilities, so that a high success rate is promoted. As the child becomes more confident and secure, within the context of the child's stamina and concentration span, experiences are offered that are at the fringes or just beyond the currently exhibited functional status. Children with PMLD tend to have low stamina so this process can be slow. There may be many relapses until the comfort zone is shifted slightly to assimilate the new sensory or communication skill.

Frustration can be a heavy burden, lowering self-esteem and contributing to depression. I believe children with PMLD should be started in an MSE type environment as young as possible to try and lessen the build up of frustration.

Pedagogical approaches

Adults influence the behaviour of children. Children also influence the behaviour of adults (Bell and Harper 1977). In particular, children with PMLD influence the behaviour of educators working in the MSE. Educators often complain that the range of pedagogical approaches they use in the MSE shrink over time. To help educators maintain an 'open-minded' view of the MSE I have developed a model which categorises pedagogical strategies for use in the MSE (Pagliano 1999). In this model activities are categorised as being either teacher-led or child-led, active or passive (see Figure 3.1). This model provides the educator with a guide to translate educator-led, passive activities into more child-led, active, activities.

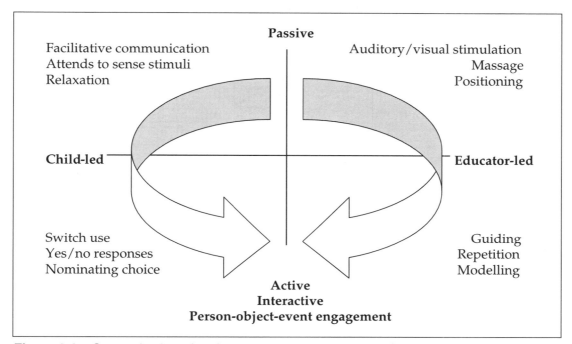

Figure 3.1 Categorisation of pedagogical strategies for the MSE

Individualised sensory programme

The individualised sensory programme (ISP) is a written statement for each child who will be using the MSE. It is designed to complement the child's individualised education plan (IEP). However, the focus for the ISP will be different from that from the IEP. The ISP contains:

- details of the child's current level of achievement in the areas of functional proprioception, functional exteroception, functional engagement and functional communication (see Appendices 2–9);
- details of how the hybrid MSE is to be set up for the child, identifying particular equipment and particular instructional strategies that will be used (see Chapter 1 and Appendices 2–9);

- details of dates and duration MSE will be in use, including which specialists will be involved, when and for how long (see Chapter 4 on the transdisciplinary team, and Appendices 2–9);
- annual recreational, therapeutic and educational goals for the MSE;
- appropriate objective evaluation procedures, with at least an annual review to determine if instructional goals have been met (see Appendix 10).

Basic principles of learning and teaching in the MSE

The MSE provides the child with a carefully constructed supportive learning environment that is matched to fit the child's sense abilities. To achieve this match educators must understand the learner, understand the learning process and know how to construct a supportive and challenging environment.

To provide effective learning in the MSE, teaching must be grounded in a comprehensive understanding of the child. This includes being aware of the child's prior experiences and respecting their influence on the child's growth and development, being aware of the child's abilities, motivation, interests, expectations, potential, learning styles as well as emotional and social well-being.

Many factors, not only the child's ability or disability, will impact on the child's learning. Other factors include the child's age and maturity, attitudes, perceptions, gender and sociocultural background. Educators using the MSE need to recognise that children with PMLD have the capacity to continually extend and refine their own knowledge, even when the learning is very slow and difficult to quantify.

Educators need to identify ways particular children learn best and to build on their learning strengths. They do this by careful observation, by identifying the child's current functional status and by using the MSE to create learning opportunities that are not too easy nor too difficult. A feedback process needs to evaluate learning outcomes and to readjust instruction accordingly. Children with PMLD have usually developed high frustration levels. It is therefore important that the MSE provides children with many opportunities for success.

All learning is multifaceted. Learning outcomes should therefore not focus only on what is learnt. They also need to be constructed in ways that provide children with opportunities to better understand the way they learn. Children with PMLD learn through doing, through being engaged and through achieving success. They learn best using concrete materials in meaningful ways. It is important that educators use the success experiences in the MSE to help the children understand that they were the ones who achieved this success and they achieved the success by doing an action. Reinforcement in the form of tangible rewards and social approval must be immediate, consistent and clear.

Children with PMLD need to not only achieve success but also be aware that they are making progress. Children learn best by linking new learning with something they already know. This is why establishing a strong knowledge base in the form of a comfort zone is so important.

At a team level, the MSE team should model an ongoing commitment to learning as a prerequisite for establishing worthwhile learning partnerships between the child and all members of the MSE team. MSE practitioners must collectively explore ways to improve learning and teaching. Team members create learning opportunities for children with PMLD through the application of their own professional expertise and practical experience. They refine and improve these learning opportunities through ongoing evaluation and through the use of critical reflection and group discussion.

On a practical level, each session with a child in the MSE should be briefly written up and kept in the child's file. Every four to six weeks depending on progress, the child's functional senses and engagement and communication should be reviewed by the MSE team. In this way the team tends to work coherently together instead of each member addressing issues in isolation. Comfort zones are very important. Comfort zones provide the child with sufficient security and confidence to accept exploration at the fringes and just beyond the zones. I feel that during exploration frustration levels must be kept well below two per cent and success well above 98 per cent if the child with PMLD is to maintain confidence and security.

At team meetings different team members take leadership in different areas according to expertise. In developing activities to provide further functional sensation, engagement and/or communication, brainstorming is a useful approach. Set approaches are often stale and not necessarily fine tunable to the individual. The programmes are built from the child out. The MSE is super flexible and the only limitation to what can be offered is the MSE team members' imagination. Follow-up and critical reflection is integral to implementing strategies.

Recreational, therapeutic and educational goals for the MSE

The recreational, therapeutic and educational goals for the MSE are going to be informed by the child's level of achievement in functional proprioception, exteroception, engagement and communication. The assessment forms in Appendices 2–9 are organised in ways that will assist the MSE team when identifying objectives. Often one objective will closely interrelate with other objectives. Appendices 2–9 are designed to be used together. At other times the MSE may be used to develop a single sense ability.

The following case studies illustrate how educational programmes may be developed using different MSE design prototypes. They illustrate a selection of practical strategies and methods that can be used in the MSE.

The white room

Kay, a six year old girl with PMLD, has been assessed as being at the stage of voluntarily engaging in reaching. Team members therefore identified 'reach to touch' as the next learning outcome to be achieved for functional proprioception. For functional touch Kay was identified as being at the early locating stage. The learning outcome for touch was therefore identified as, 'Kay will learn to replace random searches with more intentional searches'. The learning outcome for object engagement was for Kay to achieve 'increased levels of tactual orientation'. This learning outcome would be recorded as successful when Kay unambiguously showed that she had received information about an object through active touch. The learning outcome for communication was for Kay to recognise the sign for touch. Kay's ISP therefore contained four learning outcomes all related to touch.

To complicate matters, both Kay's parents and her teacher report that she is tactile defensive. This means that working out how to achieve the learning outcomes will need to be carefully thought through. Kay's assessment form identified one of her likes as the ball pit so the MSE team decided to use a white room set up using a ball pool not much bigger than Kay to see how she responded. The class teacher was asked to start just by making observations. After two weeks she said:

> There may be times in there when we're almost totally quiet and just listening to the music and enjoying the visual stimulation. For instance, my group of children goes in on a Monday during the lunch session when there's only one adult in there. Usually what I tend to do is just go over and sit nearby one of the students and look at what that student's doing with the fibre-optics display, how the student is manipulating it. We've got one little girl who – her hand movements in there on the fibre-optics are just unreal – you just don't see that in the classroom. She's not motivated to lift her arms up and explore things like she will do in there. Another girl, Kay, is very tactile defensive – she'll look at the fibre-optics but she won't touch it, yet she absolutely loves the ball pit. When she's in there sometimes she'll move her legs around and explore things and other times she just lies there quite calmly. My approach to that is just to make sure she's fine – that she's still breathing in there - and just to go over and make sure she's happy and leave her in her own little world for a while and let her enjoy that.

Here the teacher is saying she adopts a kind of laissez-faire approach where the emphasis is on enjoyment and exploring opportunities for the children to engage with equipment in ways that match their needs. The teacher says the MSE is different to the classroom because it offers a different level of motivation for the children. Even though Kay is tactile defensive she is using her legs to explore in the ball pool. The trick now is to get her to use her hands. At the meeting the team members brainstormed a number of possible strategies to try. These included:

- Changing the number of balls in the ball pool – when Kay explores the pool with her legs she will discover the floor as well as the balls.
- Changing the size of some of the balls – having big balls as well as small balls.
- Covering the ball pool with a sheet – same ball pool but with a quite different feel – maybe moving from passive touch to active touch.
- Putting sponge shapes in with the balls.

- Putting some squeaky balls in with the regular balls.
- Having clear balls to replace the coloured balls.
- Adding a light under the ball pool.

The MSE team discussed the pros and cons of each suggestion until they eventually decided to try the sheet idea (see Table 3.1).

Current level	Learning outcome	Equipment	Instructional strategy	Measurement
Functional proprioception – Voluntary reaching	Reach to touch	Ball pool	Cover ball pool with a sheet on alternate days	Child able to compare touching behaviour before and after sheet
Functional touch – Early locating	Replace random searches with more intentional searches	Ball pool	Cover ball pool with a sheet on alternate days	Child able to compare touching behaviour before and after sheet
Object engagement	Increased levels of orientation	Ball pool	Cover ball pool with a sheet on alternate days	Child unambiguously shows information received through touch
Communication – accidental communication	To recognise body sign to touch	Ball pool	When child explores using touch – sign 'good touching'	Child indicates recognition of sign 'good touching'

Table 3.1 Developing an ISP for Kay

The dark room

The following story is told by a teacher who has specialised in teaching children with visual impairment. This teacher has been using the dark room to teach visual stimulation to a ten year old boy with PMLD. The ISP has developed through ongoing use of the dark room (see Table 3.2).

Trevor has some brain damage but I don't as yet know which parts of the brain are damaged. Trevor's parents treat him as if he's totally blind. I suppose over the years they've observed him not using his vision at home and have responded accordingly. I wasn't convinced that Trevor was totally blind so I started taking him into the dark MSE. I'm now planning to invite

Trevor's parents to join us in the dark room because I want to show them that he can see, well just a teeny, weeny bit – but the important point is even though he can only see a little bit, the vision that he does have gives him pleasure. He genuinely enjoys looking at the lights. There's something very magical about our relationship with lights – there must be otherwise why would we make such a fuss with lights on special occasions?

Trevor and I go into the dark room three times a week for visual stimulation. We always go at the same time, immediately after morning tea and we spend about 15 minutes in there. I wheel him into the room with the lights on. Once he's comfortable I switch the lights off and we're in total darkness. It has really been a case of me learning by closely watching Trevor's reactions for signs that he is seeing something. I have four spot lights positioned in the four corners of the opposite wall. Each spot light is focused on to its diagonally opposite spot so the light doesn't flash into our eyes. It's not aggressive at all. I'm quite happy to look at each spot light myself. I always start by turning on the top left spot and quietly wait for Trevor to respond. Sure enough he turns his head to look at the light and then he breaks into a big smile. Even during our first visit to the dark room Trevor was able to make it very clear that he was visually aware of the light. His big smile tells me he can see the light.

The big smile also lets me know that seeing the light gives him pleasure. I just let him gaze at the spot for a little while. At first it would take Trevor about a minute but now he only needs to look for about 30 seconds and then he's ready for a new activity. He's getting much faster at attending to the visual stimulus. After the first spot I turn it off and we have a little rest with just a dim light on. During the rest time I always congratulate Trevor using both body signs and speech. I say how clever he is being able to see the light and he smiles all over again. It's the same smile! It's his special 'I can see' smile.

Next I turn on the top right hand spot and wait for him to respond. I suppose I'm now thinking about Trevor's ability to localise his vision. We do exactly the same things every time. I even use the same language – I've got it scripted. We have built up quite a routine. His ability to visually localise is also improving. We go around the room clockwise and then anticlockwise. He's getting faster at responding – that's why we are able to fit more into our fifteen minutes. I know Trevor is getting faster because I've been timing him and keeping records. The biggest difference occurred when I started explaining exactly what I was doing – using the scripted language, helping him to anticipate. I now tell him in advance where and when I'm going to start the spot. Trevor then positions his head in anticipation before I turn on the light.

You know, I think this activity is changing his expectations. When we come into the dark room he now expects to use his vision. There is such a big change in his attitude. It will be so interesting to see what his mum and dad say. They know about what we're doing because they gave their permission for me to use the dark room and I have been telling them about what we have been doing using a communication book but I think they will be surprised when they actually see it for themselves. Recently I've started to experiment with colour so I suppose we're moving on to visual recognising. I have yellow, red and blue slides I put on the spots. Trevor can see the yellow ones – no trouble – in fact I think he likes the yellow light better than the ordinary spot.

To respond to the red ones, we have to get closer – about one metre closer. He doesn't respond to the blue spot at all, not yet anyway. I'm starting to learn about Trevor's visual window to the world. I know it's very, very tiny but it's still a window and he likes looking through it. I think the activities we do help Trevor develop fluency and endurance. I haven't really checked for momentum yet. I'll probably let him practice developing his fluency for a few more weeks before I try to distract him while he is looking.

My future plan is to use a computer presentation with a data projector to present various shapes using a flicker system. I think I'll leave the blue and just use the yellow and red lights on the computer. It's a learning curve for both of us.

Current level	Learning outcome	Equipment	Instructional strategy	Measurement
Uncertain if Trevor can see?	Visual awareness	Spot light in dark room	Visit dark room 3 x 15 mins/ week Preacquisition Acquisition	Turns head to look at light, smiles
Visual awareness	Visual attending	Spotlight in the dark room	Spotlight on for 60 seconds then rest Fluency	Watches spotlight for a minute
Visual attending	Visual localising	Two spotlights in the dark	Two spotlights one top left, one top right Fluency	Moves head and eyes from top to top right to observe spotlight
Visual localising yellow	Visual recognition	Spotlights with yellow and red	Add yellow and red slides to the spotlights	Recognise and red coloured spots Fluency
Visual recognition	Visual understanding	Lights with shape flicker	To be decided…	

Table 3.2 Developing an ISP for Trevor

The grey room

The following account is by a teacher who describes how she uses the grey room:

Lex is eight years old but he looks as if he's five. He's the oldest of the six kids in my class. They all have foetal alcohol syndrome (FAS). Lex has all the classic FAS characteristics: slack jaw, thin upper lip, no ridge between his mouth and nose, wide set eyes, small and slight – and he acts like he has FAS as well. He has an intellectual impairment, and he doesn't understand the idea of boundaries, he always wants hugs, touches others in inappropriate ways, finds it difficult to concentrate, is easily distracted – loses his temper in a flash. He'll get violent with the other children or with the furniture, then has absolutely no understanding of the consequences of his behaviour.

Our classroom is pretty much stimulus free – funny idea isn't it? It's to stop Lex and the others from being distracted. Lex is so easily distracted! Everything I do is to help him concentrate. Lots of structure and repetition. I keep lessons short – no more than 15 minutes and we mainly do daily living skill activities – things that are meaningful for him.

Lex wears a weighted jacket to give him a sense of place. I work a lot on giving him a sense of place. He sits on his small square piece of plain carpet for lessons and keeps within specially drawn lines to identify what place he needs to be in for that particular lesson – otherwise Lex and the others will just wander off.

If Lex loses it, you know, his temper, which is a fairly frequent occurrence, he goes to the time out space at the back of the room to calm down – then he comes back and rejoins the activity. These children like being together so the idea of using the time out space works well because they only spend a few minutes in there and then want to return to the group.

They don't seem to mind going into the time out space. They seem to understand that it helps them calm down because they don't have the people stimulus to contend with. Actually I spend a lot of time explaining to them what I am doing.

I wouldn't use the time out space if the child was using it to avoid being part of the group. These children don't use it to avoid the other children. They use it when it's too difficult to be with other people. But then after a few minutes they're fine and they come back to the lesson.

The sound space

In the following account, a special education early childhood teacher talks about using the sound space.

My son used to love banging on the kitchen pots and pans when he was a toddler. He'd grab a spoon and bang, bang, bang. I was fascinated by the fact that he never seemed to tire of it. Do you think it's a boy thing? Anyway I thought it might be interesting to try to recreate this experience in the sound space with Jim. Jim is four years old and as far as we know he has moderate hearing loss, low vision and an intellectual impairment. Actually it didn't take long for him to catch on. I just modelled what to do for a while, pretended I was my son actually, then gave Jim some kinesthetic prompts and off he went. We've had three sessions with the pots and pans now and he bangs them like an real pro. He knows he's the one making the noise – it's something he's extremely proud of. He can make loud and very loud bangs, as well as fast and not so fast ones so he's experimenting and learning. I think the sound space makes it so much easier for Jim to listen to himself – he doesn't have to compete with all that background noise we have in the classroom. I'm not so certain I would have been able to get him banging on the pots and pans in our classroom, not in the sustained way he bangs them in the sound space anyway.

The interactive area

This is a teacher talking about using switches:

All the children in our class have PMLD but they all have some vision so we decided to celebrate Christmas by doing a visual activity in the MSE. The kids all bought in a decoration from home which we put on a tree with some Christmas lights and connected them to a big, easy-to-manipulate, switch. This meant the children could each take turns switching on the lights – the lights would stay on for one minute – so each child got about seven goes at switching on the lights during the first session. We'd put the switch on a child's wheelchair tray, make the room dark, I'd shine a torch on the switch so the child could see it clearly, the child would press the switch and the tree would light up. Each time a child switched on the lights Yvonne, my teacher's aide and I would go 'aah' and 'ooh' and all the children would smile and cheer – in their own kind of way – you could tell they loved it.

Each child seemed to be more aware of the other children than they usually are as well. I think they started connecting socially because they wanted to share their enjoyment. Anyway, the really neat thing was that some of the mums came to the MSE, they wanted to see their decoration on the tree. So we showed them what we had done and they all decided to do the same thing at home. I was so excited. Jean's mum now tells me that every night after dinner Jean switches on the Christmas tree lights at home. It has become an important family ritual.

The water area

In this account, a teacher is describing her use of the water area:

All five students in my class have PMLD with a profound physical disability – in fact they're all in wheelchairs most of the day. I take them to hydrotherapy once a week in a specially set up water area with a heated indoor pool and a jacuzzi. I'd like to take them more often but we need one adult for each child. I depend on volunteers to help me and I can only get these volunteers to come on Thursday afternoons. It's been quite hard because I have to teach them what to do and it's very labour intensive going into the pool – but well worth the effort. There's a lot of preparation – getting their swimming costumes on and going to the washroom. The children can tell they're going to the water area and they get excited. That tells me a lot about how much they like it.

Joan particularly likes it, her face lights up in anticipation, and she has a special happy sound she makes when she's being wheeled to the water area.

I'm just fascinated by the way Joan's behaviour changes when she gets in the pool. Joan doesn't move much when she's belted into her wheelchair but the moment she gets into that pool she vigorously waves her arms and kicks her legs. The pool is her world. What's really amazing is how she manages to keep up the exercise for the whole 15 minute session.

It's such good exercise for her – and for all the students. They like the freedom to move being in the water gives them. After the swim we all get in the jacuzzi for a nice, gentle water massage – that's when we are all together – it's a sharing time so our visit to the water area has a flow to it. It's good having it on Thursday afternoons because I can send them home happy, relaxed and ready for a good sleep.

Soft play

Another teacher talks about the soft play area:

Our soft play area was specially designed for young children with visual impairment and associated disabilities. Most areas consist of PVC covered foam rubber solid shapes which are joined together with velcro – so the whole room is very safe. Basically it's five metre square room divided into four smaller squares. Each square is joined by a bright yellow pathway with a red padded column in the centre of the room. One enters the room and travels clockwise around the room. You can tell the orientation and mobility teacher helped with the design. It was her idea to add tactile cues to match the colour changes around the room.

At 12 o'clock a green right-angled suspension bridge hugs the wall, with rope ladder sides that go right up to the ceiling. The bridge goes round to 3 o'clock. The bridge covers a four stepped terrace which gently slopes into a bean bag base (meant to signify water). The first step is green and the next three go from light to dark blue – so the whole room is very attractive. The second square is a giant multicoloured ball pool with green sides. The children have to climb up one step to get into the ball pool whereas they have to climb down one step to get into the lake. In the corner (at half past 4) a slippery slide gently slopes into the ball pool. The slide's parallel with the wall so it's safer. The third square is a right-angled green tunnel which goes along the wall from 6 o'clock through to 9 o'clock. The tunnel is on the same level as the yellow path. The base of the tunnel is made of a soft fur material so it's really nice to crawl through. The tunnel flanks a cubby house that can be pulled to pieces and reconstructed. It consists of four sides, one with a window and one with a door, and a two-piece slanting roof. The house has white walls, green floor and the roof is black. In the fourth square is a trampoline which has red safety sides which are the same height as the yellow path.

Julie is six years old, totally blind with an intellectual disability. She has a limited incentive to move. Her mother says when Julie visits their local playground she prefers to stay in the same place, mostly on the swing. Julie spent her first session in the soft play environment just slowly exploring the whole room which I thought was a big plus. By the end of the session she could tell me about each of the four squares and the kinds of activities you could do in each one. I think knowing where everything was helped her feel more confident about playing in it because in the second session, when she was joined by her friend Hazel who has low vision, the two of them were more adventurous. It was so lovely seeing them play in uninhibited ways. I think the room has a lot of potential.

The portable environment

Below, an advisory visiting teacher talks about developing a portable MSE:

As an advisory visiting teacher it was my job to visit children in isolated areas. Tina, one baby I worked with, was deaf blind. She was premature and had spent the first eight weeks of her life in hospital. At six months of age, all she wanted to do was lie quietly in her cot.

Mum complained that changing her and giving her a bath was very stressful. Apparently Tina would scream and scream. Even though I strongly encouraged the parents to give Tina lots of cuddles, each time I visited Tina would still be in her cot and she would still scream whenever I tried to pick her up. This worried me a lot so I decided to build a portable multisensory environment – one piece at a time.

I had a big long chat with Tina's mum and explained what I was planning to do. I got her involved in the problem solving. We began with a lamb's wool skin base. Whenever Tina went in the cot she would lie on the lamb's wool. Whenever we took her out of the cot we would place her on the lamb's wool – whether it was on the floor, in mum and dad's bed, in the car, in the pram or outside in the yard – our goal was to keep Tina near the action, near mum and dad, but content and comfortable. The lamb's wool was her comfort zone.

When I visited I would put the lamb's wool on my lap and then lie Tina on it. I would give her gentle pats and jiggle my knees. To my amazement this strategy worked – so we attached some velcro to the base and started to add things. First we added a teddy bear that her grandmother had sent as a present. She accepted the teddy bear so the following week we added a honey scented pillow to the teddy bear's pocket. Tina also accepted this so next we added another toy – one selected by her mother.

Actually it was quite a big deal – we went to the local toy shop together and we spent a good hour talking about what would be suitable. Tina's parents began to collect new things to add to extend her portable MSE. I think a big break through happened when Tina started to like being pushed around in the pram. I got mum and dad to keep the pram moving backwards and forwards, taking it up and down steps, jiggling it up and down – anything that would provide some proprioceptive stimulation.

The virtual environment

The following is from a technology teacher, describing virtual games:

I'm certain virtual reality will be a lot more prevalent in the future but even now VR is part of most people's lives – just visit any games arcade. You can become a racing car driver, or fly a helicopter, drive a space shuttle, a speed boat, even a fire engine. People with disabilities can participate. Often it only takes a minimal change to the controls to ensure that the child with a disability can join in the fun. My favourite is a roller coaster ride which has a switch control. All the child has to do is press the switch to start the ride and release the switch to stop the ride. It's a hoot!

The inclusive area

In this account, a special education teacher supports the inclusion of children with disabilities in a mainstream primary school, and discusses play areas:

Now that so many children with disabilities attend regular schools it is important that schools design play areas to include all children, not just the able bodied ones. Play areas need to be designed to include all children from the start of the design process. Whenever a child with a disability is enrolled at the schools I visit, I spend time with the child checking out the various play areas in the school. This ensures that the child has a good understanding of the play areas and enables me to write up a report on the suitability of the play areas for the school administration. I see my report as a legal document so I take this report very seriously indeed.

Here is my checklist:
- What age group is this playground designed for?
- What features make this playground suitable for this age group?
- Which groups of children in the school are allowed to play in this playground, and at what times?
- Are particular groups of children excluded? Why? When?

- Would a child with the following impairment (describe) ....
  (learning difficulty, intellectual, hearing, physical, visual, communication, social/emotional, multiple) be able to play in this area? If not what would it take to make the area more suitable? Why?

- What equipment would be suitable? Why?
- What equipment would not be suitable? Why?
- What areas might be dangerous? What makes them dangerous?
- How could problem spots be fixed?
- What additions would make the playground more suitable?

- What special instructions does the teacher on playground duty need to be given? Remember if you have a child with a disability in your area while you are on duty it means increased duty of care is required for that child.

The pluralist environment

A special school teacher describes a pluralist MSE:

A group of Aboriginal and Torres Strait Islander students from our local Technical and Further Education (TAFE) College who were enrolled in their art course offered to paint some murals for our special school. We have several indigenous children with PMLD at our school so we suggested the TAFE students paint four panels for our MSE. They based the panels on Australian animals: kangaroo, emu, honey ant and dugong.

When the panels were completed and added to the room I was surprised how striking they looked. We liked the room so much we decided to have an official opening. We invited the parents of our indigenous students and the TAFE student artists to a special function. It was just for them.

At the function we played Aboriginal and Torres Strait Islander music, which was provided by one of the parents, and a guest performer read out stories from the dreaming. Several parents were so impressed they offered to help with future sessions. This was the first time we have had indigenous parents volunteering to work at the school.

Previously I don't think the parents were made to feel welcome. Now with the new panels in the MSE the parents seem to feel more a part of the school and that is good for the children. The parents can see how happy their children are in the MSE. The TAFE students were absolutely delighted to see their work make such an impact. It was a win, win situation.

The social space

In my previous interview with you I really liked your description of the MSE being their 'pub'.

Yes I still think the MSE is their pub or their night club. Young adults I know spend a lot of time together socially, but our students, they are the same age yet they have no concept of what it's like going to a proper disco or a night club. We need to be thinking about their experiences and equating them with age-appropriate activities. I think it's their social space and that is an important reason for having an MSE.

So do you think their socialisation skills have developed because of the MSE?

I don't know because I have never gone out with them on their trips outside the school. So I can't comment on that one. I don't go out into the community with them. That would be something that the teachers and the aides would do and it would be interesting to know if there was something that mirrored the same thing in the MSE and they saw the students react – to keep that as record. After that, no I don't know.

Some staff have said they thought that the students seemed to be more open to other students in the MSE than they are in the classroom and in the community, they're looking at other students, smiling more etc.

Yes I think that definitely does happen. And one of the things is that a lot of our students live in supported accommodation and they tend to look to the adults for their interaction so they miss out on that interaction with their peers. I think it's very interesting how in the MSE the students don't look to the adults for their interaction, they look to each other and to me that's something very important, when they interact with students of their own age.

Have you got any particular stories to illustrate that point?

Well I think of one boy who is a loner, very much a loner, and whenever he's in the classroom he just wants to be by himself – he'll even push his wheelchair away from the others. In the MSE he will not touch other students, but he will look at them and he will lie close to them on the floor. Whereas at any other time he doesn't – not at all. And he doesn't look at other students in the classroom so something social is happening in the MSE. I think, the students know it's theirs, it's their space, it's for them. Not only for them as an individual but for them as a group, which is totally different to being in a room which is just for one child.

Code of ethics

A code of ethics to inform use of the MSE is a set of statements about appropriate and expected behaviour of team members in the MSE. The code is based on agreed upon values so it is important for team members to work together to develop a code that they think is suitable. Essentially a code of ethics provides a set of principles and aims which guide professional decision making.

1.   The primary responsibility of MSE team members is to value and promote the education, safety and wellbeing of children who use the MSE.
2.   MSE team members should maintain a commitment to parents and families of children with PMLD.
3.   MSE team members should strive to support and assist each other in ways that build trusting, collaborative relationships.

Summary

An instructional strategy is a broad approach to teaching. Instructional methods describe the specific actions of the MSE team when teaching. The idea of matching task difficulty to sense ability is an instructional strategy used in the MSE. The instructional method is the procedure by which this strategy is implemented.

The MSE is built from the child out. The goal is to make the child's world more meaningful. To do this, MSE design must take account of the child's sense abilities, personality, temperament, interests, likes and dislikes, degree of engagement and communication skills as well as age and sociocultural background. Many children with PMLD have such wide ranging learning difficulties that they require individualised techniques, such as some form of simplified tactile body language, in order to communicate.

When a child first enters the MSE the educator starts the activity by establishing a comfort zone for the child using sense experiences that are familiar and acceptable to the child. The comfort zone is physically constructed before the child comes into the room. The child is settled into the comfort zone using a scripted auditory and tactual commentary to enrich the experience and to provide a basis for communication development. Once two comfort zones have been established, the child can explore the MSE by moving from one comfort zone to the next under the guidance of the facilitator. An important principle of MSE use is to ensure that the children have as much success and as little frustration as possible while extending their functional status. Success will occur when there is a perfect match between the demands of the environment, the child's ability and the task difficulty.

One problem that often occurs in the MSE is that the range of pedagogical approaches used by educators gradually decrease over time. I have developed a model which categorises pedagogical strategies as either teacher-led or child-led, passive or active. This helps educators maintain a pedagogically 'open-minded' or expanded view of MSE use. Educators can use this model to translate passive, educator-led activities into active, child-led activities.

The individualised sensory programme is a written statement for each student who will be using the MSE. It is designed to complement the student's IEP and includes details of the child's achievement, in particular sense development, short- and long-term learning outcomes, details about the most suitable equipment and environment, details of the amount and type of professional support and evaluation procedures.

Basic principles for learning and teaching in the MSE are elucidated. Regular assessment and critical review by the MSE team is vital. Brainstorming helps to develop the next set of instructional strategies and methods.

A series of vignettes is presented to illustrate practical instructional strategies and methods that can be used in each of the MSE design prototypes. A code of ethics predicates the actions of the MSE team.

4 Programme-environment-individual fit in the MSE

Introduction

The MSE is designed to assist children with environmental learning difficulties to effectively engage in tasks that match and extend their ability. Educators are interested in obtaining information about the children's sense windows to the world. The exceptional multisensory needs of the children inform MSE design, construction and ongoing use. The best way to obtain such information is by working in teams.

The team

Three team types used in education are the multidisciplinary, the interdisciplinary and the transdisciplinary team. All three teams comprise members from different disciplines, but differ in the level of collaboration that is possible. The transdisciplinary team provides the best support infrastructure for the MSE because it allows for more sophisticated levels of collaboration.

Collaboration is defined by Friend and Cook (1992) as 'a style for direct interaction between at least two coequal parties voluntarily engaged in shared decision making as they work toward a common goal' (p. 5). The authors identify six characteristics of collaboration as: equality of participants, voluntary involvement, need for a common goal, joint responsibility for participation and decision making, joint sharing of resources, and joint accountability of outcomes. Successful collaboration is valued by participants as a style of interaction. Through collaboration participants develop increased levels of mutual trust and form a cooperative working community.

The **multidisciplinary** team is the traditional team approach used in special schools. It involves the least amount of collaboration. Team members work independently within their own area of specialisation. They conduct their own assessment, write their own reports, do their own planning, provide their own service and chart their client's progress in their area of specialisation. MSEs are usually located in special schools so the same multidisciplinary team that is used elsewhere in the school continues to be used in the MSE. Multidisciplinary teams develop when the school has a token staff of therapists who work at the school on a part time basis, or when therapists are employed by a different authority (e.g. the Health Department).

Individual multidisciplinary team members may regard the MSE as a single function space (e.g. the teacher thinks it is for education, the therapist thinks it is for therapy). Team members may or may not have been involved in the planning of the MSE. In fact the MSE may be a rigid space, designed and built by a commercial firm. The way an individual team member constructs the MSE determines the type of activities that member is willing to conduct in the space. For example, a teacher might say, 'I never put Sandra in the ball pool because I don't know whether it would be suitable for her. She has a rod in her back.' The teacher rules out the ball pool as an educational tool because of lack of access to physiotherapy details, even though a physiotherapist might be on the staff at the school. This low level of communication is a major problem with multidisciplinary teams. It often results in the inadvertent exclusion of parents as well.

The **interdisciplinary** team consists of members who continue to work independently within their own area of specialisation but they do meet informally to discuss issues before they conduct their own assessment and write up their reports. Team members also meet to discuss their reports before they move into the planning stage, so the services they provide, although still primarily within their own area of specialisation, are more interrelated than in the multidisciplinary team. In the interdisciplinary team parents are regarded as contributors. In an MSE run by an interdisciplinary team, the teacher may still work independently with students but the teacher is more aware of what the therapists might be doing and why. For example, the teacher may have consulted with the physiotherapist regarding how to position Sandra in the ball pool but still lacks the confidence to put Sandra in the ball pool on her own, just in case something goes wrong. 'Sandra has had three operations on her back in the past three years. I think it's too difficult to introduce Sandra to the ball pool. I'd rather leave it. I don't want to take the responsibility, besides the physiotherapist will work with her later.' Interdisciplinary team members consult with each other but continue to maintain clear boundaries regarding their work roles (teachers teach, therapists provide therapy).

The **transdisciplinary** team uses the greatest amount of collaboration. Team members work outside the traditional boundaries of their specialisation and that means their roles are constantly changing depending on the needs of the child. They conduct preliminary discussions in preparation for joint evaluation. Collaborative assessment informs the development of a joint service plan which is then implemented by a primary service provider who charts the student's progress. Parents are equal members of the team and may become a primary service provider. If the MSE is run by a transdisciplinary team then the MSE reaches its full potential as an 'open-minded' space. Teachers, therapists, parents and caregivers work together to make things happen for the student that would otherwise not have been possible. For transdisciplinary teams to work there needs to be a **manager**, someone to coordinate and organise the team. It is also important that all members maintain a high level of commitment to making the team effective.

Having a transdisciplinary team means Sandra can play in the ball pool. The physiotherapist works with the teacher to plan a safe way to move and position Sandra in the ball pool. After several goes at transferring Sandra in and out of the ball pool with the physiotherapist's help, the teacher feels sufficiently confident to be able to do it without assistance. With that hurdle out of the way, the teacher then wants to actively involve Sandra in the ball pool. At present Sandra is lying on her back looking up at the ceiling. She is enjoying the new sensation of being in the ball pool but she is not playing with the balls. The team calls on the occupational therapist who comes up with a new plan. This time a bean bag chair is placed in the empty ball pool, Sandra is put on the bean bag in a seated position, then the balls are added. Sandra is now positioned in a way that enables her to use her hands. When reflecting on the developments with Sandra the teacher might comment, 'You know, if I was just working by myself, Sandra would still be spending her time in the MSE on a mattress, on the water bed or in her wheelchair. I would not have been game to put her in the ball pool.'

When all members of the transdisciplinary team are involved in the MSE from the start the team is able to design the MSE they want and the redesigning becomes an ongoing process – one thing leads to another. For example, even though Sandra was positioned in a way that allowed her to move her hands, she was not using them as much as desired by the team in its movement learning objective. When Sandra's mother brought in Sandra's teddy bear from home, the team placed the teddy bear in the ball pool just in front of Sandra. This was the right incentive because Sandra reached to grasp, to pick the bear up. Everyone felt that Sandra had made significant progress. Here the assessment is tightly integrated with the process of using the MSE.

Team members

Membership of the MSE team is going to change over time depending on the particular needs of particular children and the school's overall resources. For example the MSE designer may be involved during the initial design and implementation phase but then may only return to the team if significant changes are required to the design. Optimum team size is thought to be between five and seven. If the team gets bigger than this it can become unwieldy.

Core members usually include: child, parents or caregivers, significant teachers (class teacher, specialist teachers), teacher's aide, physiotherapist, occupational therapist, speech language pathologist and designer. Other members could include a nurse, an orientation and mobility specialist and a volunteer (see Table 4.1).

Role	Job description	Transdisciplinary focus in MSE
Child (student)	To engage (with objects, people, events), make choices, learn skills of daily living, be productive/ active, enjoy human creativity, communicate, become self-determining.	Build MSE from child out. Involve child in making MSE-related decisions. Identify child's ability profile, interests, communication dictionary.
Parent (caregiver)	Lives with child therefore likely to know child best – able to identify child's abilities and needs. Able to build on, extend and link work done at school with other parts of child's life – able to provide feedback re short- and long-term effectiveness of school programmes.	Provide input re: • child's ability, interests, communication skills • MSE goals and objectives • ways to link MSE activities to home and community and vice versa • feedback re short- and long-term effectiveness of MSE.
Designer	Specialises in disability-specific interior and exterior design, visual arts, architecture, industrial design, design technology, environments for play, leisure, recreation, therapy and learning.	Manages initial design and implementation process – collects ability profile of users and discipline specific MSE information from all team members.
Teacher * Often the manager	Responsible for educational programme of individual students. Identifies educational goals including short-term instructional objectives, educational services to be provided, and appropriate evaluation criteria.	Ensures MSE design/use maximises opportunities for learning and development. Responsible for MSE educational programme for each individual student.
Speech language pathologist	Responsible for child's communication programme. Evaluates, diagnoses and treats speech and language disorders. Assesses quality and quantity of speech sounds and/or augmentative and alternative communication symbols. Teaches and evaluates.	Ensures MSE design/use maximises opportunities for development of communication skills.

continued

Role	Job description	Transdisciplinary focus in MSE
Occupational therapist	Specialises in development and maintenance of functions and skills necessary for daily living, especially fine motor ability. Prescribes and administers treatments involved in developing adaptive skills.	Ensures MSE design maximises opportunities for learning and development of functions and skills necessary for daily living
Physiotherapist	Specialises in development and maintenance of physical ability – develops exercises for relaxation, stimulation, strengthen muscle groups, improve balance, bear weight, gross motor skills.	Ensures MSE design maximises opportunities for child to improve personal quality of life by achieving optimal physical potential.
Teacher's aide	A paid employee who works alongside and under the direction of the class teacher.	Plays an active role in MSE functioning at the day to day level by helping in activities associated with education, therapy or relaxation.
Volunteer	Unpaid individual who provides nonpaid services. Ensure person is appropriate by obtaining references and conducting an indepth interview. Volunteers usually work under the direction of other team members.	May play an active role in MSE functioning at the day to day level by helping in activities associated with education, therapy or relaxation.

Table 4.1   Potential transdisciplinary MSE team members

Programme-environment-individual fit in the MSE

Programme-environment-individual fit involves making a three way match between what the child needs to learn, the learning outcomes or tasks, the learning environment and the child's ability. This three way match involves identifying:

- what the child can do at present;
- what learning outcomes we want the child to achieve in the MSE;
- why these outcomes need to be achieved;
- how these outcomes will be achieved in the MSE.

Decisions have to be made in regard to the type of MSE to be used and how this environment will be used to achieve the identified learning outcomes. It is important to recognise that the principal uses of the MSE, for leisure, therapy and education all overlap to a greater or lesser extent.

I believe that depression in children with PMLD is much more common than is generally acknowledged. I also believe that many children with PMLD are much more fearful of their environment than is generally acknowledged in the literature. I think that one of the most important roles of the MSE is to simply get a child ready to want to learn. This is achieved by providing an emotionally supportive environment that enables the child to feel confident and secure, by establishing a comfort zone for the child.

This open-minded aspect, where relaxation, therapy and education overlap is why collaboration between users of the MSE is so vital. The match is clearly dependent on the child's current level of attainment. In deciding on an intervention, past experience helps to inform future initiatives. The last step in making a match is to review performance, both of the child and the intervention. Desired outcomes need to be delineated and the extent to which these outcomes are being met over time assessed. This is the basis of accountability.

Accountability

The precise measurement of learning outcomes has become an important part of education for all children. A major shift in focus in the education of children with disabilities from one of access to one of standards occurred in the USA on 4 June 1997. The amendments:

> … require that states develop alternative assessments for those students unable to participate in the regular state or district assessment programs, that guidelines for determining who should be included in alternate assessments, and that the performance of students taking alternate assessments be reported.
>
> (Ysseldyke *et al.* 1998, pp. 1–2)

This change of focus from process to outcomes has now been adopted in most western countries.

Accountability systems developed for mainstream education do not fit easily into the MSE. The MSE is not a classroom where the teacher is traditionally in charge, nor is it a clinic, the traditional work space of the therapist. It is a flexible space which is open for collaborative use by teachers, therapists, parents and caregivers. Measurement of outcomes in the open-minded MSE is therefore different to the classroom. It is compounded by the challenges imposed by the student's disability, the involvement of stakeholders from disciplines other than education, and the expansion of learning outcomes to include therapeutic and recreational goals. The MSE therefore provides another space for the student to explore, another space to learn new skills or practise old ones which were previously learnt in the classroom, in a clinic or at home.

Accountability involves keeping a record of our actions. We do this by preparing a report or description of what we have been doing. This information is examined to identify advantages and disadvantages, and to make judgements to justify the value of the work we have been doing. It is the process by which we catalogue reasons to show us how we have acted responsibly. We need this information to assist us to develop, monitor and review our education programmes, to improve our service, and to report to parents, caregivers, employers and the community at large.

Integrating assessment with instruction

Success in the MSE is evaluated by systematically identifying the extent to which desired results or outcomes are being achieved. This involves listing the child's current achievements, specifying desired outcomes and assessing the extent to which these outcomes are being met over time.

The following outcomes-based accountability system provides a procedure which the MSE team can follow when using the MSE. Check that it is:

- involving *all* members of the trandisciplinary team (student, parent, teacher, physiotherapist, occupational therapist, speech language pathologist, other) in *all* phases of the process;
- defining essential terms carefully to ensure that all team members are speaking the same language;
- deciding *why* outcomes need to be measured;
- deciding *what* outcomes need to be measured;
- defining *what* particular behaviour indicators represent success for each particular outcome for each particular student;
- defining *how* and *when* these indicators will be measured and by *which* member of the transdisciplinary team.

The following is a case study to show how the system might work. Of course this case study is just one example of the way one team worked together to come up with a programme-environment fit for one individual student. The programme-environment-individual fit is going to be different for each child who uses the MSE. The case study, however, does help to illustrate how the MSE team can work together over time to achieve particular outcomes.

Gary

Gary is a 12 year old youth with profound multiple disabilities. Gary cannot walk but he can sit when supported in his wheelchair. He cannot talk nor sign but he is able to show that he likes or dislikes something by either refusing to or agreeing to cooperate.

Gary has some vision and some hearing but he does not use either sense very much. For example he will pick up a yellow Smartie if it is placed on the desk in front of him and he will sometimes respond if there is a loud noise but, often he does not. Recently a long time habit has started to cause serious problems. Gary sucks his fist. He shoves his fist deep in his mouth and sucks on it whenever he gets the opportunity – which lately has been most of the time. Even though Gary has had an outbreak of sores around his mouth which are raw and inflamed he continues to suck his fist.

Members of Gary's transdisciplinary team consist of Gary's carer Susan, Tracey the school nurse, Helen the physiotherapist, Wayne the occupational therapist, Julianne the speech language pathologist, Annette the class teacher and case manager, and Ingrid the teacher's aide and secretary. They have met to discuss the problem of Gary sucking his fist. Wayne and Helen have only seen Gary once so far this year. Julianne, who is new to the school staff, has been working with Annette and Ingrid to introduce a more effective communication system for Gary, using body signs. The meeting, of which the following is an account, was held during week eight of term one.

Annette, the teacher, brought the meeting to attention, saying:

I'd like to welcome you all here today to discuss the problem of Gary's fist sucking. Has anyone got anything they would like to say about Gary to start the meeting?

Tracey, the school nurse, offered: *I'm very concerned with the sores around Gary's mouth and I want the team's approval to attach a splint to both Gary's arms to prevent him from putting his hands in his mouth, at least until his sores are healed, which could be several weeks. Susan, if possible I'd like to keep the splints on Gary while he's at home too. What do you think?*

Susan the carer hesitated, then said, *OK ... but I feel the splints need to be a temporary solution. I think we should be trying other things as well.*

Hear, hear agreed Helen, the physio. *It's not good for Gary to have the splints on all the time. He needs to exercise his arms – but it's a problem, I agree. Gary still sucks his hands when I'm doing joint movement work on his legs. I can't stop him.*

Annette summed up, noting the nods of various team members: *So it sounds like everyone is concerned about Gary sucking his fist.* Annette continued: *I've found this accountability system for use in the MSE. It consists of a series of questions aimed to help us focus on the issues. They say we need to begin by defining Gary's behaviour. We all need to agree that we are talking about the same thing. Would someone be willing to define Gary's behaviour?*

Wayne the OT volunteered: *Gary's sucking is a highly repetitive action. It's irrelevant to activities outside him and it provides him with predictable feedback so I would describe it as a stereotyped behaviour.*

Annette: *Does everyone agree with defining Gary's behaviour as stereotyped behaviour?*

Tracey: *Yes but more than that. It is stereotyped behaviour but Gary's sucking is now so compulsive, so frequent and so intense that it has resulted in an outbreak of sores all around his mouth. His whole mouth area is raw and inflamed. It's definitely challenging behaviour because he's doing damage to himself. It's also challenging behaviour because the sores seriously limit his ability to mix with his peers. They take one look at the sores on his face and they avoid him.*

Wayne: *Yes Tracey is right. I only see Gary occasionally so I hadn't really thought about his sucking as being as serious as this. I had assumed it was just self-stimulation – but I agree he is injuring himself and his injuries do make it more difficult for him to use community facilities.*

Annette, checking the group for consensus: *So we're all agreed Gary's sucking can be defined as challenging behaviour. Now on to the next question. When does he suck his fist?*

Susan: *I hadn't actually thought about it as challenging behaviour either Wayne, but the fact is, at home Gary sucks his fist whenever he's not otherwise occupied. Really the only times he doesn't do it is when he's asleep – and that's because I pull his fist out of his mouth just before I go to bed. Oh, and he doesn't suck it at meal times and during activities he enjoys, like bathing, getting dressed and having a massage.*

Annette: *Would everyone agree this provides a fair indication of how often Gary sucks his fist?*

Ingrid: *He seems to suck his fist less often when he is in his comfort zone. For the last two weeks Annette and I have been establishing the mattress in the corner as one of Gary's comfort zones. The mattress is near the bubble tube so there's the sound of bubbles. We chose colours that Gary likes – a red velvet throw for the mattress and a yellow pillow case. We deliberately chose a smell that Gary likes. One that is arousing rather than relaxing. Gary has his own pillow and the pillow case has a scent pocket sewn into it. I add the fresh peppermint satchel just before we go into the MSE. It's his external comfort zone rather than the internal one I think he retreats to when he sucks his fist and lies in a foetal position. The routine of the body signs, the smell, the textures, the colours and the words, they are much more important than I initially realised when we set it up. They all help to construct and to maintain it as an external comfort zone. Annette and I have made up a form for everyone. This is probably a good time to give it out. You can see we follow a five step scripted process to establish the comfort zone.* (Hands form out.) This is the form:

1. Feet. Guide Gary's feet to touch the velvet cover and mattress underneath – say and body sign simultaneously 'Feet touch bed.'
2. Hands. Guide Gary's hands to touch the mattress – say 'Hands touch bed.'
3. Nose. Touch Gary's nose and tap the satchel – say and body sign 'Nose smells peppermint.' Tactile finger spell PEP for peppermint.
4. Ears. Touch Gary's ears – say and body sign 'Ears hear bubble tube.' Body sign bubble.
5. Eyes. Touch Gary's eyes – say and body sign 'Eyes see red bed. Eyes see yellow pillow.'

Annette: *What sense system do you think the sucking behaviour stimulates?*
Ingrid: *Taste?*

Helen, jokingly: *I don't think the experience would be very tasty – not unless someone is putting honey on his fist. I think taste would be a very minimal part of the stimulus.*

Julianne: *He's getting lots of proprioceptive feedback, and the mouth is very tactile. I think he would be getting both proprioceptive and tactile feedback. I'm certain Gary finds the activity very comforting.*

Annette: *That leads us very nicely onto the next question – it's more difficult – I'll be interested to hear what you think. What things cause Gary to stop sucking?*

Wayne: *Gary stops sucking his fist when he's asleep or he starts to engage with the outside world, with an object, a person or an event.*

Annette: *Does anyone want to add to this?*

Julianne: *Gary stops sucking his fist when his engagement with the outside world makes him feel comfortable. I think the fist sucking provides Gary with a way to switch on a feeling of comfort. Sure he stops sucking when he engages with the outside world but only when this engagement is making him feel comfortable. If he doesn't feel comfortable he'll continue to suck his fist. Actually I think we're seeing a dramatic increase in the sucking behaviour at present because he's starting to go through puberty and he has so few communication skills. He's finding life particularly frustrating at present. Julianne added. So I think it's tied in with communication.*

Annette: *So what activities could we try in the MSE to encourage Gary to stop being self-engaged?*

Julianne: *We need to work from Gary's comfort zones.*

Wayne: *Gary could stay in his comfort zone and manipulate the big blue switch. I could connect it to a light tower. Gary could push the switch for the light to shine. If I set the timer for the light to shine for 20 seconds, then if he wants it to come back on, he would have to press the switch again. I'd probably lie him on his tummy and get him to look up. Prone position's a good viewing position and it'd make it harder for him to suck his hands. It would also get his muscles working. The most important outcome at this stage though, would, of course, be whether Gary actually stopped sucking his fist – and for how long.*

Annette: *Sounds good Wayne. Our next job is to decide why these outcomes need to be measured.*

Wayne: *Outcomes are measured to let us know if the activity is successful.*

Susan: *You know what? Apart from the comfort thing I also think Gary just needs more brain food at the moment. It really started during the school holidays. It's much more difficult to keep him active at home. I like these sessions because they give me ideas to use with Gary at home.*

Julianne: *I'd support this hypothesis. I think it's a combination of comfort, being frustrated with inability to communicate and lack of stimulation so it might be a good idea if we all came up with a plan to help Gary achieve more stimulation, not just Wayne.*

Annette: *I agree Julianne, so we need to decide what outcomes to measure, what particular behaviour indicators represent success for each outcome, how and when these indicators will be measured and by which member of the transdisciplinary team.*

Wayne: *I think we should just focus on measuring the amount of time Gary is engaging in purposeful behaviour as opposed to sucking his fist.*

Ingrid: *I could work with each of you in the MSE. That would provide some continuity. I'll meet with each of you and we can come up with a strategy similar to Wayne's. Once we get Gary in his comfort zone we could take his splint off and try to keep him from sucking his hand by engaging him with the particular activities you choose. I could record the length of time we are able to keep Gary engaged while each of you focuses on keeping Gary occupied. What about we meet back again in a fortnight's time to compare notes?*

At the meeting two weeks later, the following discussion took place:

Annette: *Welcome back everyone. Ingrid's been keeping me up to date and I'd like to start by congratulating you all. Gary's face has cleared up a lot. I must say he looks a lot more handsome without sores all around his mouth. I think he feels a lot better without them too. He was laughing quite a lot today in the ball pool which is such a positive change.*

Susan: *He's been laughing more at home too.*

Annette: *I'd like to hear your reports. What about we go around the circle.*

Helen: *Usually I work with Gary doing his joint range movements in the classroom. I lie him on a mattress I bring in and he sucks his fist while I work on his legs. Then he alternates fists in mouth while I work on his arms and shoulders. If I don't let him suck his fist he gets upset. For the last two sessions I have used the red mattress and the yellow pillow in the MSE. Ingrid's been helping me set it up. We follow the comfort zone steps. Then we put the music on and start the lighting – the oil slide and the pin spot on the disco ball and when he's comfortable I exercise his legs keeping his splints on. On both occasions by the time I got to his arms he was so comfortable and relaxed he didn't need to suck his fist so I kept the splints off. During the first session we were splint free and without sucking for 10 minutes and during the second session for 12 minutes. I must say I was pleasantly surprised.*

Wayne: *Ingrid and I tried the light tower using the set-up I described last meeting. Gary was not that keen to lie on his stomach so it took us 25 minutes to set him up in prone position. That meant we only had 5 minutes of splint free light switching and watching – but once he started doing it he really liked it. Then during the second session he was much more cooperative. The light switching was extended to 10 minutes – so I was quite pleased. I think we learnt a lot, didn't we Ingrid?*

Julianne: *I was so impressed with the way you put Sandra in the ball pool, Wayne, I decided to try Gary in the same set-up. I suppose we have made the ball pool comfort zone number two. Ingrid and I have prepared a five point set-up for Gary in the ball pool which I'll give to you all later. He had a wonderful time in the ball pool. During both my sessions he handed me quite a few balls and did not suck his fist until close to the end of the session. The first time was 10 minutes of object-person-engagement and the second a whopping 15 minutes.*

Susan: *At home I've been taking the splints off when I put him in the bath – adding red bubble bath, it has a strawberry smell, and putting toys in the water. His favourite is a yellow rubber duck – sucks it I'm afraid but at least he hasn't been sucking his hands. Before anyone says something, I know a yellow rubber duck is not really age-appropriate and I'm looking for a better toy but I haven't found one yet – I want a yellow aeroplane or a yellow submarine. Actually with bath time, drying, massage and dinner yesterday we went for a full hour without hands in the mouth. Two weeks ago I would never have dreamed that was possible so I'd like to thank you all for working with me on this one.*

Annette: *So it seems what you're saying is, the best way to keep Gary from sucking his fist is to keep him actively engaged with meaningful stimulation, to work from his comfort zones and to emphasise the communication – and the programme in the MSE seems to be helping. It's really nice to hear that what we've been doing in the MSE has had some benefit for what has been happening at home. Unfortunately keeping him actively engaged is a full time job for at least one adult. How do you think we should follow up now? We can't all spare this amount of time to just work with Gary one-to-one.*

Commentary

Several points arise from this case study. To begin with, the case study is by no means an example of best practice. The case study is simply an example to help illustrate how a transdisciplinary team might use the MSE and particularly to focus on the idea of integrating assessment with instruction. There are a number of worthwhile features to the team work. There is also considerable room for improvement. For example:

1. Using the MSE is not easy. The team may be made up of a motivated group of experts but members have to work hard at using the MSE.
2. All team members need to ensure that they speak a common language. They achieve this by acknowledging that different disciplines define terms in different ways. The team therefore needs to come up with its own definitions which everyone agrees on.
3. As well as being a challenging behaviour Gary's fist sucking has also become a problem behaviour because the sucking provides a barrier to learning.
4. Participating in the transdisciplinary team is time consuming. Wayne had not put in the time needed to be able to fully participate. He had not established sufficient rapport with Gary to realise that his sucking had become both a problem and a challenging behaviour. Furthermore he did not have a sufficiently good rapport with Gary to be able to set up the light tower activity as quickly as he thought he could. When therapists work with children with PMLD for short periods, say 30 minutes each month they often do not get to develop a close working relationship with that child. It might have been better for Wayne to have spent the first session reinforcing the comfort zone and improving his relationship with Gary before moving on to the switch activity.
5. Gains made can be very tiny. It is therefore very important to consider gains within a context of priorities. Julianne has been helping to develop a set of priorities with communication at the top of the list.
6. Should Annette, the class teacher and case manager, have spent more time and effort ensuring that all members of the team had access to a more solid information base before the meeting? Where was Gary's individualised education plan and how did the focus on his fist sucking fit into the whole picture? Annette really needed to be showing much more leadership with instructional strategies and educational methods.
7. Ingrid the teacher's aide has the fewest academic qualifications and the least amount of professional training, yet she is the one who has been left to do the most work with Gary.
8. Helen, the physiotherapist has been focusing on joint range measurements. Was this the most appropriate action? Should she have shown more leadership in the area of developing Gary's functional proprioception? Who polices the experts? Who challenges the team? Joining the transdisciplinary

team may mean that the old boundaries that distinguish certain disciplines from others need to be broken down. This can be threatening and can result in a steep learning curve for all team members.

9. Were all members of the MSE team made to feel equal? What about Helen's comment to Ingrid? I realise Helen meant it as a joke but was it also a put down to keep Ingrid in her place? If so, then it could make it more difficult for the team to work together as equals.

10. There is considerable need for members of the transdisciplinary team to engage in critical personal reflection. Unless time for such reflection is timetabled in this is unlikely to happen.

11. What things do you think the team might try next?

Such a transdisciplinary team approach is limited in the real world by under-funding of disability services. However, not supporting parents/caregivers to the greatest extent possible also entails a heavy cost. At its best, the MSE can be an environmental bridge to the wider world. Construction of the bridge by the MSE team requires careful, thoughtful, methodical planning. This book has highlighted the issues involved.

Summary

Collaboration is defined by Friend and Cook (1992) as 'a style for direct interaction between at least two coequal parties voluntarily engaged in shared decision making as they work toward a common goal'. The level of collaboration defines three types of MSE team: multidisciplinary, interdisciplinary and transdisciplinary. The transdisciplinary team is the most evolved. MSE team membership may include: the child, parents or caregivers, significant teachers (class teacher, specialist teachers), teacher's aide, physiotherapist, occupational therapist, speech language pathologist and designer. The programme-environment-individual fit involves identifying what the child can do at present; what learning outcomes we want the child to achieve in the MSE; why these outcomes need to be achieved; and how these outcomes will be achieved in the MSE. An outcomes based accountability system involves all the members of the MSE team, defining terms carefully, programme-environment-individual fit and deciding when and by which team members outcomes will be measured. These points are illustrated in an extended vignette about Gary followed by a commentary.

Appendix 1

Multisensory Environments – Information Sheet

A variety of equipment is on hand to provide visual, auditory, olfactory, tactile and kinesthetic [movement] stimulation. These stimuli include a wide range of pleasant aromas, soothing music, vibrating cushions, tactile wall panels, wind chimes, wooden flying birds, beanbags, a water bed, a ball pit, and two giant clear perspex pillars of water with ever-rising air bubbles. A wheel-effect optikinetics projector makes fluid oil patterns that slowly slide across two walls. A touch-responsive plasma light sculpture sits invitingly in one corner and a fibre-optic spray cascades light-like water down another. Two spot lights shine on a first clockwise then anticlockwise rotating disco mirror ball while ultraviolet light bounces off neon iridescent flowers, earth globe mobiles, stars and planets, and long, hanging coloured tapes. (Pagliano 1999, pp. 3–4)

Even though each MSE is different, the above description does give you some idea of what a MSE is like, particularly for a child.

Children with profound multiple learning difficulties (PMLD) experience difficulties developing a relationship between themselves and the external environment. This is because the way they learn about the world at large, namely through their senses, is impaired in some way. Helping children with PMLD develop better relationships with themselves and the world at large therefore involves organising the environment in ways that are meaningful for them.

The multisensory environment (MSE) is a room or space where stimulation can be controlled, manipulated, intensified, reduced, presented in isolation or combination, packaged for active or passive interaction, and time-matched to fit the perceived motivation, interests, leisure, relaxation, therapeutic and/or educational needs of the user.

When using the MSE the focus is on finding ways to make sense information more meaningful to the child. This is a complicated process. It requires the involvement of a team of specialists including parents or caregivers. Development of the MSE involves four steps.

1. Find out as much information as possible about the way the child actually uses his or her senses. Information is obtained through close and ongoing observation of the child in a variety of environments. This includes:

    • interviewing the parents or caregivers;
    • collecting all up-to-date medical assessments that relate to the child's sense development;

- ensuring that the child has up-to-date prosthetic devices if necessary, such as spectacles, hearing aids and others;
- obtaining assessment reports from all relevant specialists: the class teacher, the physiotherapist, the occupational therapist and the speech language pathologist.

2. The team works out ways to match the environment to the child's abilities. For example, the mother might have noticed that the child, who otherwise does not use his vision, seems to relate to the colour yellow, especially in bright light. The team might therefore decide to use a bright yellow bowl for all meals. Once a number of environmental and ability matches have been identified, the team designs an individualised sensory environment.

3. The team develops a programme for use in the MSE. The team decides what the child needs to learn. The team decides how this learning is going to take place (the pedagogy or method of teaching). Putting it together is the programme-environment-individual fit.

4. The programme-environment-individual fit is put into action. The emphasis is on utilising the child's abilities and the environment in ways that aid and support development and learning. This requires the use of ongoing assessment.

You can read more about MSEs in:

Pagliano, P. (1999) *Multisensory Environments.* London: David Fulton Publishers.

Pagliano, P. (2001) *Using a Multisensory Environment: A Practical Guide for Teachers.* London: David Fulton Publishers.

MSE Parent/Caregiver Questionnaire

Name of child:
Date of birth:
Name(s) of parent(s)/caregiver(s) being interviewed:

Address(es):

Contact details:

Person conducting the interview:

Date interview completed:

Social details
Who lives with the child?

Who often sees the child?

Who occasionally sees the child?

Draw the child's family tree showing extended and blended family, ages, occupations, significant attributes:

Who are the most important figures in the child's life?

What are the most important places in the child's life?

What have been the most important events in the child's life?

What services does the child currently receive? Give full details.

Who are the child's doctor(s)? Give names/addresses/contact details.

Who are the child's therapist(s)? Give names/addresses/contact details.

History
When did you first know there were problems?
What happened then? (Attach sheet if necessary.)

Checklist	
Medical history and current status	
	Birth details
	Vaccinations
	Serious illnesses
	Operations
	Medications
	Allergies

Checklist	
Sensorimotor development, history and current status	
	Motor
	Balance
	Smell
	Taste
	Touch
	Hearing
	Vision
	Communication skills

Personality/ Temperament
How would you describe your child's personality?

Please mark where you think your child's personality is along these four scales:

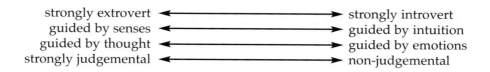

strongly extrovert ⟷ strongly introvert
guided by senses ⟷ guided by intuition
guided by thought ⟷ guided by emotions
strongly judgemental ⟷ non-judgemental

Please mark where you think your child's temperament is along these nine scales:

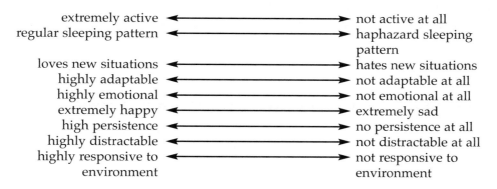

extremely active ⟷ not active at all
regular sleeping pattern ⟷ haphazard sleeping pattern
loves new situations ⟷ hates new situations
highly adaptable ⟷ not adaptable at all
highly emotional ⟷ not emotional at all
extremely happy ⟷ extremely sad
high persistence ⟷ no persistence at all
highly distractable ⟷ not distractable at all
highly responsive to environment ⟷ not responsive to environment

Comments:

Tell me about your child's interests, likes and dislikes.

Other issues
What are your hopes, fears, concerns for your child, both now and in the long term?

How do you feel a MSE will help your child?

Other relevant information:

Signature:_____

Appendix 3

Functional Proprioception

Name of child:
Date of birth:
Person conducting assessment:
Date assessment completed:

Physiotherapist's report: ATTACHED / NOT ATTACHED
Progress report on issues highlighted in previous report and not addressed above:

Skill level reached in activity proposed in previous functional proprioception report.

	Skill level	Comments
	Preacquisition	
	Acquisition	
	Fluency	
	Endurance	
	Momentum	
	Generalisation	
	Adaptation	
	Retention	
	Maintenance	

Current status:
1) Which describes the child's current level of sensorimotor development?

	Extension against gravity	
	Lifting trunk and straightening trunk in prone position	
	Lifting trunk and straightening trunk in supine position	
	Limb movements	
	Random	
	Bilateral arms together	
	Bilateral legs together	
	R L	Arm and leg together, same side (circle)
	R+L L+R	Arm and leg together, different sides (circle)

	Body movement through space
	Front – back
	Side to side
	Rotary
	Using support for balancing
	Lying
	Sitting
	Crawling
	Standing
	Walking

2) Which proprioceptive activities are popular with the child?

	Ball pool
	Rocking
	Spinning
	Swaying
	Swimming pool
	Swinging
	Water bed
	Others

3) What movements will the child voluntarily engage in, in the MSE?

	Reach
	Reach to touch
	Grasp
	Reach to grasp
	Hand(touch)-eye coordination
	Release

New issues:
Design an activity for the child that will further facilitate muscle use and the development of strength, mobility and stability.

Identify anticipated activity intensity, frequency and duration:

Identify any special resources/personnel that will be required:

What will be the motivation for this activity?

What outcome, that is positive and meaningful for the child, will result?

How will this outcome be measured?

Follow-up plan:

Other comments:

Signature:_____

Functional Taste and Smell

Name of child:
Date of birth:
Person conducting assessment:
Date assessment completed:

Progress report on issues highlighted in previous report:

Skill level reached in activity proposed in previous functional taste and smell report.

	Skill level	Comments
	Preacquisition	
	Acquisition	
	Fluency	
	Endurance	
	Momentum	
	Generalisation	
	Adaptation	
	Retention	
	Maintenance	

Current status:
1) Observe and comment on the child's ability to:

Suck	
Chew	
Swallow	

2) Eating/drinking preferences:

Favourite food(s)
Favourite drink(s)
Which foods refuses to eat
—Suggestions why?

Which drinks refuses to drink
—Suggestions why?

3) Update on the child's taste and smell likes and dislikes:

Tastes				Comments
Sweet (honey)	☺	☺	☹	
Sweet (sugar)	☺	☺	☹	
Salt (anchovies)	☺	☺	☹	
Salt (crisps)	☺	☺	☹	
Sour (lemon juice)	☺	☺	☹	
Sour (grapefruit piece)	☺	☺	☹	
Bitter (angostura bitters)	☺	☺	☹	
Bitter (endive)	☺	☺	☹	
Soft textures (yoghurt)	☺	☺	☹	
Solid textures (apple)	☺	☺	☹	
Cold (ice cream)	☺	☺	☹	
Room temperature (water)	☺	☺	☹	
Warm temperature (custard)	☺	☺	☹	
Chilli (mild chilli beans)	☺	☺	☹	
Milk (cold)	☺	☺	☹	
Orange juice (room temperature)	☺	☺	☹	
Chocolate drink (warm)	☺	☺	☹	

Smells				Comments
Basil (arousing)	☺	☺	☹	
Chamomile (relaxing)	☺	☺	☹	
Cinnamon (arousing)	☺	☺	☹	
Clary sage (arousing)	☺	☺	☹	
Eucalyptus (relaxing)	☺	☺	☹	
Frankincense (relaxing)	☺	☺	☹	
Lavender (relaxing)	☺	☺	☹	
Lemon (arousing)	☺	☺	☹	
Patchouli (arousing)	☺	☺	☹	
Peppermint (arousing)	☺	☺	☹	
Rose (relaxing)	☺	☺	☹	
Rosemary (arousing)	☺	☺	☹	
Ylang-ylang (relaxing)	☺	☺	☹	

Other smells and taste experiences _____ Comments

           ☺   😐   ☹

           ☺   😐   ☹

           ☺   😐   ☹

           ☺   😐   ☹

4) What taste and smell skill level has the child reached?

	Taste and smell skill level	Comments
	Taste/smell awareness	
	Taste/smell attending	
	Taste/smell localising	
	Taste/smell recognition	
	Taste/smell understanding	

New Issues:

Describe an activity for the child that will further develop functional taste and smell.

Identify the anticipated intensity, duration and frequency of new chemosensation experience.

Identify any special equipment/personnel that will be required.

103

What will be the motivation for this activity?

What outcome, that is positive and meaningful for the child, will result? How will the outcome be measured?

Follow-up plan:

Other comments:

Signature:_____

Appendix 5

Functional Touch

Name of child:
Date of birth:
Person conducting assessment:
Date assessment completed:

Occupational therapist's report: ATTACHED / NOT ATTACHED

Progress report on issues highlighted in previous report and not addressed above:

Skill level reached in activity proposed in previous functional touch report.

	Skill level	**Comments**
	Preacquisition	
	Acquisition	
	Fluency	
	Endurance	
	Momentum	
	Generalisation	
	Adaptation	
	Retention	
	Maintenance	

Current status:
1) Is the child ready to begin tactual development?

Does the child require more work in functional proprioception?

Is the child showing evidence of tactile defensiveness or tactile avoidance? If so give examples.

2) What tactual stage has the child reached?

	Locating – random or intentional search for object
	Exploring object
	Manipulation of object
	Recognition of object tactually
	Comparison - showing preference or rejection of objects
	Communication - using object to signal
	Organising - set place/ task for objects

3) Update on the child's touch likes and dislikes

Comments

Textures (rough to smooth)

Coarse sandpaper   ☺ 😐 ☹

Velvet   ☺ 😐 ☹

Density (hard to soft)

Glass   ☺ 😐 ☹

Sponge   ☺ 😐 ☹

State (gas to fluid to solid)

Fan   ☺ 😐 ☹

Milk   ☺ 😐 ☹

Apple   ☺ 😐 ☹

Surface to depth (palpation)

Feel something with gloves on   ☺ 😐 ☹

Size (small to large)   ☺ 😐 ☹

Sand   ☺ 😐 ☹

Rocks   ☺ 😐 ☹

Temperature (hot to cold)

Hot water bottle   ☺ 😐 ☹

Ice   ☺ 😐 ☹

Vibration (static, gentle, vigorous)

Vibrator – stopped   ☺ 😐 ☹

Vibrator – slow   ☺ 😐 ☹

Vibrator – fast   ☺ 😐 ☹

Shape (circle, square)   ☺ 😐 ☹

Other touch experiences

    ☺ 😐 ☹

    ☺ 😐 ☹

    ☺ 😐 ☹

    ☺ 😐 ☹

New Issues:
Describe an activity for the child to further develop functional touch.

Identify the anticipated intensity, duration and frequency of this activity.

Identify any special equipment/personnel that will be required.

What will be the motivation to try this activity?

What outcome, that is positive and meaningful for the child, will result? How will the outcome be measured?

Follow-up plan:

Other comments:

Signature:_____

Functional Hearing

Name of child:
Date of birth:
Person conducting assessment:
Date assessment completed:

Audiologist's report: ATTACHED / NOT ATTACHED
Otorhinolaryngologist's report: ATTACHED / NOT ATTACHED
School file (hearing issues):   ATTACHED / NOT ATTACHED

Degree of hearing loss		Educationally deaf (no functional hearing)
		Hard of hearing
		Limited hearing
Type of hearing loss		Conductive loss
		Sensorineural hearing loss
		Mixed hearing loss
		Central / cortical hearing loss

Progress notes on issues highlighted in previous report, not addressed above:

Skill level reached in activity proposed in previous functional hearing report.

	Skill level	Comments
	Preacquisition	
	Acquisition	
	Fluency	
	Endurance	
	Momentum	
	Generalisation	
	Adaptation	
	Retention	
	Maintenance	

Current status:
1) What aids have been prescribed to help hearing? Is the child wearing/using them?

2) What is the best listening environment for the child?

Checklist	
	Time of day
	Volume
	Pitch
	Length of listening
	Background noise
	Concurrent MSE activity

3) What auditory skill level has the child reached?

	Auditory skill level	Comments
	Auditory awareness	
	Auditory attending	
	Auditory localising	
	Auditory recognition	
	Auditory understanding	

New issues:
Describe an activity for the child to further develop auditory functioning.

Identify the anticipated intensity, duration and frequency of use of the activity.

109

Identify any special equipment/personnel that will be required.

What will be the motivation to use this activity?

What outcome, that is positive and meaningful for the child, will result? How will the outcome be measured?

Follow-up plan:

Other comments:

Signature:_____

Functional Vision

Name of child:
Date of birth:
Person conducting assessment:
Date assessment completed:

Optometrist's report:	ATTACHED / NOT ATTACHED
Ophthalmologist's report:	ATTACHED / NOT ATTACHED
School file (vision issues):	ATTACHED / NOT ATTACHED

Degree of vision loss		Educationally blind (no functional vision)
		Low vision
		Visually limited
Type of vision loss		Field of vision
		Distance visual acuity
		Near visual acuity
		Stereopsis
		Colour vision
		Accommodation/fusional vergence
		Ocular motility: saccades, tracking
		Near point of convergence
		Cortical visual impairment

Progress notes on issues highlighted in previous report, not addressed above:

Skill level reached in activity proposed in previous functional vision report.

	Skill level	Comments
	Preacquisition	
	Acquisition	
	Fluency	
	Endurance	
	Momentum	
	Generalisation	
	Adaptation	
	Retention	
	Maintenance	

Current status:

1) What aids have been prescribed to help vision? Is the child wearing/using them?

2) What is the best visual environment for the child?

	Checklist
	Time of day
	Image size and intensity
	Image location and complexity
	Colours
	Lighting
	Background stimuli
	Movement
	Length of viewing
	Concurrent MSE activity

3) What visual skill level has the child reached?

	Visual skill level	Comments
	Visual awareness	
	Visual attending	
	Visual localising	
	Visual recognition	
	Visual understanding	

New issues:
Describe an activity for the child to further develop visual functioning.

Identify the anticipated intensity, duration and frequency of use of the activity.

Identify any special equipment/personnel that will be required.

What will be the motivation to use this activity?

What outcome, that is positive and meaningful for the child, will result? How will the outcome be measured?

Follow-up plan:

Other comments:

Signature:_____

Functional Engagement

Name of child:
Date of birth:
Person conducting assessment:
Date assessment completed:

Progress notes on issues highlighted in previous report:

Skill level reached in activity proposed in previous engagement report.

	Skill level	Comments
	Preacquisition	
	Acquisition	
	Fluency	
	Endurance	
	Momentum	
	Generalisation	
	Adaptation	
	Retention	
	Maintenance	

Current Status:
1) Does the child show any of the following stereotyped behaviours?
SS = self-stimulation, adverse sequelae unlikely
P = problem behaviour, interfering with learning and development
C = challenging behaviour, resulting in injury to persons and/or property and/or community exclusion

Analyse child's behaviour in terms of:
• **Intensity:** mild, moderate, severe
• **Frequency:** infrequent, moderately frequent, frequent
• **Duration:** short periods, medium periods, long periods
• **Consequence:** positive, no discernible consequence, negative – to self, others, property.

Behaviour	SS	P	C	Comments:
1. bouncing on feet or seat				
2. breathing pattern that is radically altered				
3. clothing manipulated				
4. collects and hides things				
5. contortions of body parts involving tight sustained flexions				
6. feet tapping on floor, wall, object				
7. finger flicks (not related to eyes)				
8. grimace - corners of mouth drawn down to reveal upper teeth				
9. hand vigorously rubs mouth, face, nose, ears, hair, clothes, or objects				
10. hand wringing - rubbing and clutching each other				
11. hands locked behind head				
12. hands moved with continuous flexion and extension				
13. knocking body parts together – ankles, knees, legs, wrists, hands, arms				
14. mouthing of objects (holding non-edible objects in contact with the mouth)				
15. pica - placing inedible item (cloth, paper) into the mouth				
16. picks up scraps, threads, hair from floor, other surfaces, off other people				
17. rearranges furniture or objects				
18. rhythmic manipulation of objects by rubbing, rotating, tapping with fingers or body part				
19. rocking				
20. rumination – constantly chewing				
21. saliva swishing audibly in mouth				

continued

Behaviour	SS	P	C	Comments:
22. spins on equipment (chair)				
23. spins while standing				
24. sways head				
25. sways torso				
26. teeth clicking – audibly and rapidly closing teeth together				
27. tongue rolling and clicking				
28. touches self, objects, others				
29. vomiting				
30. makes repetitive non-speech sounds				
31. screams not obviously related to distress				
32. verbal abuse				
33. bends, bites, grabs, hits, kicks, pinches, punches, slaps, throws, twists object				
34. bites, grabs, hits, kicks, pinches, punches, pushes, scratches, slaps others				
35. chokes others				
36. hair pulling				
37. spits at others				
38. throws objects at people				
39. air swallowing				
40. bites, grabs, hits, pinches, punches, slaps self				
41. body to object banging				
42. cutting self with tools				
43. choking self				
44. drinking to extreme				
45. ear pulling, gouging, pressing on with hands, twisting				
46. eye poking, gouging, pressing with hand				
47. hair removal				
48. head punching/slapping				
49. lip chewing				
50. nail removing				
51. puts fingers in cavities				

continued

116

Behaviour	SS	P	C	Comments:
52. puts objects in cavities				
53. skin picking				
54. teeth banging				
55. teeth grinding				
56. manipulates objects in a ritualistic way – spins, twirls				
57. ritualistic head, arm movements				
58. masturbates in public				
59. touches others in inappropriate ways				
60. anal/oral behaviour in public				
61. eye crossing				
62. eye gazing or staring (fixed glassy eye look)				
63. eye rubbing, patting, scratching				
64. fingers flicked in front of eyes				
65. hands waving vertically or horizontally with fingers outstretched in front of eyes				

3) Level of engagement – with object, person or event

Level		Comments
Orientation		Basic awareness – passive
	Has information about offer to engage been received?	
	Does child stop self-stimulation in response to offer to engage?	
Responsiveness		Basic awareness – active
	Does child respond to received sense information?	
	Is the response positive, neutral or negative?	
Reciprocation		Interchange
	Is there an interchange of interaction – turn taking	
Initiative		Adding new information
	Is the child adding new information?	
Association		Internalising the interaction
	Is child making a connection of some kind – generalising, aware of object permanence, linking people and events.	

New issues:

Describe an activity for the child to further develop his/her level of engagement.

Identify the anticipated intensity, duration and frequency of use of the activity.

Identify any special equipment/personnel that will be required.

What will be the motivation to use this activity?

What outcome, that is positive and meaningful for the child, will result? How will the outcome be measured?

Follow-up plan:

Other comments:

Signature:_____

Appendix 9

Functional Communication

Name of child:
Date of birth:
Person conducting assessment:
Date assessment completed:

Speech language pathologist's report: ATTACHED / NOT ATTACHED

Progress notes on issues highlighted in previous report, not addressed above (including success/failure of communication strategies developed in previous report):

Skill level reached in activity proposed in previous communication report.

	Skill level	Comments
	Preacquisition	
	Acquisition	
	Fluency	
	Endurance	
	Momentum	
	Generalisation	
	Adaptation	
	Retention	
	Maintenance	

Current status:
1) How does the child show?

Yes	
No	
Choice	
Enjoyment	
Displeasure	

2) Update of communication portfolio
A = accidental communication, reflex action, no awareness of own action
P = pre-intentional communication, limited awareness of own action
I = intentional communication, child is proactive

Observed communication	A	P	I	Possible significance (social aspects, context)

Comments:

New issues:
Describe an activity for the child to further develop communication.

Identify the anticipated intensity, duration and frequency of use of the activity.

Identify any special equipment/personnel that will be required.

What will be the motivation to use this activity?

What outcome, that is positive and meaningful for the child, will result? How will the outcome be measured?

Follow-up plan:

Other comments:

Signature:_____

121

References

Aitken, S. and Buultjens, M. (1992) *Vision for Doing: Assessing Functional Vision of Learners who are Multiply Disabled.* Edinburgh: Moray House.

Alchin, A. and Pagliano, P. (1988) 'The parent checklist: how effective is it in isolating children with vision problems?' in *Toy Libraries and Special Education Working Together: Proceedings of the AASE (Qld) Conference.* Cairns: Australian Association of Special Education.

Bell, R. O. and Harper, L. V. (1977) *Child Effects on Adults.* New York, NY: John Wiley.

Bly, L. (1983) *Components of Normal Development During the First Year of Life and Adnormal Development,* Monograph. Oak Park, IL: Neurodevelopmental Treatment Association.

Bozic, N. (1997) 'Constructing the room: multisensory rooms in educational contexts', *European Journal of Special Needs Education* **12**(1), 54–70.

Brannock, G. and Golding, L. (2000) *The Six Step Method of Teaching Orientation and Mobility.* Brisbane, Australia: Education Queensland.

Bromley, S. M. (2000) 'Smell and taste disorders: A primary care approach', *American Family Physician,* 15 January.

Bunning, K. (1996) *Development of an 'Individualised Sensory Environment' for Adults with Learning Difficulties and an Evaluation of its Effects on their Interactive Behaviours.* Unpublished Thesis (London: City University).

Bunning, K. (1998) 'To engage or not to engage? Affecting the interactions of learning disabled adults', *International Journal of Language and Communication Disorders* **33**, 368–91.

Carey, W. B. and McDevitt, S. C. (1978) 'Revision of the Infant Temperament Questionnaire', *Pediatrics* **61**, 375–9.

Emerson, E. *et al.* (1988) *The Special Development Team: Developing Services for People with Severe Learning Difficulties and Challenging Behaviour.* Canterbury: University of Kent.

Friend, M. P. and Cook, L. (1992) *Interactions: Collaboration Skills for School Professionals.* New York, NY: Longman.

Fruchterman, J. R. (1999) The Age of Magic. http://www.csun.edu/cod/vr92.html California State University, accessed 27/10/1999.

Hall, A. and Bailey, I. (1989) 'A model for training vision functioning', *Journal of Visual Impairment and Blindness* **83**, 390–6.

Hirstwood, R. and Gray, M. (1995) *A Practical Guide to the Use of Multi-Sensory Rooms.* Leicestershire, UK: Toys for the Handicapped.

Hirstwood, R. and Smith, C. (1996) 'Developing competencies in multi-sensory rooms', in Bozic, N. and Murdoch, H. (eds) *Learning Through Interaction: Technology and Children with Multiple Disabilities,* 83–91. London: David Fulton Publishers.

Hopkins, P. and Willetts, D. (1993) 'And also ...', *Eye Contact* **6**, 26.

Hulsegge and Verheul's (1986 original Dutch edition; 1987 English translation by Alink R.) *Snoezelen: Another World: A Practical Book of Sensory Experience Environments for the Mentally Handicapped.* Chesterfield, UK: ROMPA.

Joint, S. (2001) *Tactile Signs for Students who are Deafblind and/or Multi-sensory Impaired.* Brisbane, Australia: Education Queensland.

Kewin, J. (1991) 'Snoezelen – pulling the strands together', in Hutchinson, R. (ed.) *The Whittington Hall Snoezelen Project: A Report From Inception to the End of the First Twelve Months.* Chesterfield: North Derbyshire Health Authority.

Kingwell, M. (2000) *The World We Want: Virtue, Vice and the Good Citizen.* Toronto, Ontario: Viking, Penguin Books Canada Ltd.

Kozloff, M. A. and Rice, J. S. (1998) Parent and Family Issues: Stress and Knowledge, http://www/uncwll.edu/people/kozloffm/familyautism.html accessed 11/3/2001.

Lanier, J. (1999) Virtual Reality and Persons with Disabilities. http://www.csun.edu/cod/vr92.html California State University, accessed 28/10/1999.

Linder, T. (1990) *Transdisciplinary Play Based Assessment.* Baltimore, MD: Paul H. Brookes.

Macquarie Concise Dictionary, 3rd edn. (1997) Sydney, Australia: The Macquarie Library Pty Ltd, Macquarie University.

Mount, H. and Cavet, J. (1995) 'Multisensory environments: an exploration of their potential for young people with profound and multiple learning difficulties', *British Journal of Special Education* **22**, 53–5.

Myers, I. B. and McCaulley, M. H. (1998) *Manual: A Guide to the Development and Use of the Myers-Briggs Type Indicator*, 3rd edn. Palo Alto, CA: Consulting Psychologist Press.

Neisworth, J. T. and Bagnato, S. J. (1988) 'Assessment in early childhood special education: A typology of dependent measures', in Odom, S. L. and Karnes, M. B. (eds) *Early Intervention for Infants and Children with Handicaps: An Empirical Base*, 23-51. Baltimore, MD: Paul H. Brookes Publishing.

Nielsen, L. (1994) 'The Essef board: facilitating the child's learning to stand and walk', *Information Exchange,* December, 22–23.

Pagliano, P. J. (1998) 'The multi-sensory environment: an open minded space', *British Journal of Visual Impairment* **16**, 105–9.

Pagliano, P. J. (1999) *Multisensory Environments.* London: David Fulton Publishers.

Pagliano, P. J. (2000) 'Designing the multisensory environment' *PMLD Link* **12**(2), 2–5.

Philp, M. (2000) 'The promise of hope', *The Globe and Mail*, 11 November, A14–15.

Polloway, E. A. *et al.* (2001) *Strategies for Teaching Learners with Special Needs*, 7th edn. Upper Saddle River, NJ: Merrill Prentice-Hall.

Porter, J. and Miller. O. (2000) 'Developing the use of multisensory environments' ,*PMLD Link* **12**(2), 8–11.

Power, D. (1998) 'Deaf and hard of hearing students', in Ashman, A. and Elkins, J. *Eduacating Children with Special Needs*, 3rd edn. Sydney, Australia: Prentice-Hall.

Rogers, R. (1997) 'This is tomorrow', The Sunday Review, *Independent on Sunday* 23 November, 10–16.

Smith, M. and Levack, N. (1996) *Teaching Students with Visual and Multiple Impairments: A Resource Guide.* Austin, TX: Texas School for the Blind and Visually Impaired.

Super, D. E. (1957) *The Psychology of Careers.* New York: Harper Collins.

Turner, W. D. *et al.* (1996) *Research in Developmental Disabilities* **17**(4), 312.

White, G. and Telec, F. (1998) 'Birth to school', in Kelley, P. and Gale, G. (eds) *Towards Excellence: Effective Education for Students with Vision Impairments*, 103–17, Parramatta, NSW: North Rocks Press.

Ysseldyke, J. E. *et al.* (1998). *Accountability for the result of educating students with disabilities: Assessment conference report on the new assessment provisions of the 1997 Amendments to the Individuals with Disabilities Education Act.* Published by the National Center on Educational Outcomes in collaboration with: Council of Chief State School Officers (CCSO) and the National Association of State Directors of Special Education (NASDSE).

Index